THE MINOR PROPHETS

The Minor Prophets

THE MEN AND THEIR MESSAGES

G. CAMPBELL MORGAN

FLEMING H. REVELL COMPANY
OLD TAPPAN, NEW JERSEY

Library of Congress Catalog Card Number: 60–5500

Printed in the United States of America

INTRODUCTION

THROUGH THESE PAGES runs the excitement of discovery: this is "new Morgan," in the sense that it appears for the first time in book form. Delivered originally at the famous Northfield Conference, these messages were recorded only in the *Northfield Echoes* in 1902-03, and seemed fated to be lost there from human sight and use, as just another "volume of forgotten lore."

Dr. Morgan wrote only one other book on the minor prophets; his *Voices of Twelve Hebrew Prophets,* published only in Scotland and England. This work concentrated upon one verse from each prophet. Our new book is much more comprehensive; it covers the entire prophecy of each of the twelve minor prophets—minor only because of the brevity of their writings, in comparison with those of the "major" Isaiah, Jeremiah, Ezekiel and Daniel.

To Dr. Morgan there was not much "minor" about these immortal twelve. He says in his chapter on Zephaniah: "What is the message for us as well as for Israel? What are the great truths that we may take hold of and apply to our own day and generation? What are the things here that our own souls must learn, and that are to abide with us in our living, and in our work? The notes that come to me out of the proph(ecies) are these: (1) Love's passionate anger; (2) love's patient purpose; and (3) love's ultimate victory. You may think that this is always the same message: Love. Exactly so. That is the supreme revelation of the minor prophets to my soul. The only message I find whenever I come to the close of one of these prophecies is something about God's love. When I decided to take up these minor prophets, I expected to study a very magnificent section of prophecy in which I should hear stern, hard, magnificent Hebrew prophets thundering against sin. I found this even more than I had expected, but the supreme thing in every one of their prophecies is that the God with whom these men were intimate was known by them to be a God of tender love, of infinite compassion, angry because He loves, dealing in wrath upon the basis of His love, and proceeding through judgment to the ultimate purpose of His heart. It is the heartbeat of God that throbs through these passages."

. . . *and* the heartbeat of G. Campbell Morgan!

THE PUBLISHERS

CONTENTS

THE MINOR PROPHETS

CHAPTER 1

HOSEA

CHAPTER 1

1 The word of the Lord that came unto Hosea, the son of Beeri, in the days of Uzziah, Jotham, Ahaz, and Hezekiah, kings of Judah, and in the days of Jeroboam the son of Joash, king of Israel.

2 The beginning of the word of the Lord by Hosea. And the Lord said to Hosea, Go, take unto thee a wife of whoredoms and children of whoredoms: for the land hath committed great whoredom, departing from the Lord.

3 So he went and took Gomer the daughter of Diblaim; which conceived, and bare him a son.

4 And the Lord said unto him, Call his name Jezreel; for yet a little while, and I will avenge the blood of Jezreel upon the house of Jehu, and will cause to cease the kingdom of the house of Israel.

5 And it shall come to pass at that day, that I will break the bow of Israel in the valley of Jezreel.

6 And she conceived again, and bare a daughter. And God said unto him, Call her name Lo-ruhamah: for I will no more have mercy upon the house of Israel; but I will utterly take them away.

7 But I will have mercy upon the house of Judah, and will save them by the Lord their God, and will not save them by bow, nor by sword, nor by battle, by horses, nor by horsemen.

8 Now when she had weaned Lo-ruhamah, she conceived, and bare a son.

9 Then said God, Call his name Lo-ammi: for ye are not my people, and I will not be your God.

10 Yet the number of the children of Israel shall be as the sand of the sea, which cannot be measured nor numbered; and it shall come to pass, that in the place where it was said unto them, Ye are not my people, there it shall be said unto them, Ye are the sons of the living God.

11 Then shall the children of Judah and the children of Israel be gathered together, and appoint themselves one head, and they shall come up out of the land: for great shall be the day of Jezreel.

CHAPTER 2

1 Say ye unto your brethren, Ammi; and to your sisters, Ruhamah.

2 Plead with your mother, plead; for she is not my wife, neither am I her husband: let her therefore put away her whoredoms out of her sight,

and her adulteries from between her breasts;

3 Lest I strip her naked, and set her as in the day that she was born, and make her as a wilderness, and set her like a dry land, and slay her with thirst.

4 And I will not have mercy upon her children; for they be the children of whoredoms.

5 For their mother hath played the harlot: she that conceived them hath done shamefully; for she said, I will go after my lovers, that give me my bread and my water, my wool and my flax, mine oil and my drink.

6 Therefore, behold, I will hedge up thy ways with thorns, and make a wall, that she shall not find her paths.

7 And she shall follow after her lovers, but she shall not overtake them; and she shall seek them, but shall not find them: then shall she say, I will go and return to my first husband; for then was it better with me than now.

8 For she did not know that I gave her corn, and wine, and oil, and multiplied her silver and gold, which they prepared for Baal.

9 Therefore will I return, and take away my corn in the time thereof, and my wine in the season thereof, and will recover my wool and my flax given to cover her nakedness.

10 And now will I discover her lewdness in the sight of her lovers, and none shall deliver her out of mine hand.

11 I will also cause all her mirth to cease, her feast days, her new moons, and her sabbaths, and all her solemn feasts.

12 And I will destroy her vines and her fig trees, whereof she hath said, These are my rewards that my lovers have given me: and I will make them a forest, and the beasts of the field shall eat them.

13 And I will visit upon her the days of Baalim, wherein she burned incense to them, and she decked herself with her earrings and her jewels, and she went after her lovers, and forgat me, saith the Lord.

14 Therefore, behold, I will allure her, and bring her into the wilderness, and speak comfortably unto her.

15 And I will give her her vineyards from thence, and the valley of Achor for a door of hope: and she shall sing there, as in the days of her youth, and as in the day when she came up out of the land of Egypt.

16 And it shall be at that day, saith the Lord, that thou shalt call me Ishi; and shalt call me no more Baali.

17 For I will take away the names of Baalim out of her mouth, and they shall no more be remembered by their name.

18 And in that day will I make a covenant for them with the beasts of the field, and with the fowls of heaven, and with the creeping things of the ground: and I will break the bow and the sword and the battle out of the earth, and will make them to lie down safely.

19 And I will betroth thee unto me for ever; yea, I will betroth thee unto me in righteousness, and in judgment, and in loving-kindness, and in mercies.

20 I will even betroth thee unto me in faithfulness: and thou shalt know the Lord.

21 And it shall come to pass in that day, I will hear, saith the Lord, I will hear the heavens, and they shall hear the earth;

22 And the earth shall hear the corn, and the wine, and the oil; and they shall hear Jezreel.

23 And I will sow her unto me in the earth: and I will have mercy upon her that had not obtained mercy; and I will say to them which were not my people, Thou art my people; and they shall say, Thou art my God.

CHAPTER 3

1 Then said the Lord unto me, Go yet, love a woman beloved of her friend, yet an adulteress, according to the love of the Lord toward the children of Israel, who look to other gods, and love flagons of wine.

2 So I bought her to me for fifteen pieces of silver, and for a homer of barley, and a half homer of barley:

3 And I said unto her, Thou shalt abide for me many days; thou shalt not play the harlot, and thou shalt not be for another man: so will I also be for thee.

4 For the children of Israel shall abide many days without a king, and without a prince, and without a sacrifice, and without an image, and without an ephod, and without teraphim:

5 Afterward shall the children of Israel return, and seek the Lord their God, and David their king; and shall fear the Lord and his goodness in the latter days.

CHAPTER 4

1 Hear the word of the Lord, ye children of Israel: for the Lord hath a controversy with the inhabitants of the land, because there is no truth, nor mercy, nor knowledge of God in the land.

2 By swearing, and lying, and killing, and stealing, and committing adultery, they break out, and blood toucheth blood.

3 Therefore shall the land mourn, and every one that dwelleth therein shall languish, with the beasts of the field, and with the fowls of heaven; yea, the fishes of the sea also shall be taken away.

4 Yet let no man strive, nor reprove another: for thy people are as they that strive with the priest.

5 Therefore shalt thou fall in the day, and the prophet also shall fall with thee in the night, and I will destroy thy mother.

6 My people are destroyed for lack of knowledge: because thou hast rejected knowledge, I will also reject thee, that thou shalt be no priest to me: seeing thou hast forgotten the law of thy God, I will also forget thy children.

7 As they were increased, so they sinned against me: therefore will I change their glory into shame.

8 They eat up the sin of my people, and they set their heart on their iniquity.

9 And there shall be, like people, like priest: and I will punish them for their ways, and reward them their doings.

10 For they shall eat, and not have enough: they shall commit whoredom, and shall not increase: because they have left off to take heed to the Lord.

11 Whoredom and wine and new wine take away the heart.

12 My people ask counsel at their stocks, and their staff declareth unto them: for the spirit of whoredoms hath caused them to err, and they have gone a whoring from under their God.

13 They sacrifice upon the tops of the mountains, and burn incense upon the hills, under oaks and poplars and elms, because the shadow thereof is good: therefore your daughters shall commit whoredom, and your spouses shall commit adultery.

14 I will not punish your daughters when they commit whoredom, nor your spouses when they commit adultery: for themselves are separated with whores, and they sacrifice with harlots: therefore the people that doth not understand shall fall.

15 Though thou, Israel, play the harlot, yet let not Judah offend; and come not ye unto Gilgal, neither go ye up to Beth-aven, nor swear, The Lord liveth.

16 For Israel slideth back as a backsliding heifer: now the Lord

will feed them as a lamb in a large place.

17 Ephraim is joined to idols: let him alone.

18 Their drink is sour: they have committed whoredom continually: her rulers with shame do love, Give ye.

19 The wind hath bound her up in her wings, and they shall be ashamed because of their sacrifices.

CHAPTER 5

1 Hear ye this, O priests; and hearken, ye house of Israel; and give ye ear, O house of the king; for judgment is toward you, because ye have been a snare on Mizpah, and a net spread upon Tabor.

2 And the revolters are profound to make slaughter, though I have been a rebuker of them all.

3 I know Ephraim, and Israel is not hid from me: for now, O Ephraim, thou committest whoredom, and Israel is defiled.

4 They will not frame their doings to turn unto their God: for the spirit of whoredoms is in the midst of them, and they have not known the Lord.

5 And the pride of Israel doth testify to his face: therefore shall Israel and Ephraim fall in their iniquity; Judah also shall fall with them.

6 They shall go with their flocks and with their herds to seek the Lord; but they shall not find him; he hath withdrawn himself from them.

7 They have dealt treacherously against the Lord; for they have begotten strange children: now shall a month devour them with their portions.

8 Blow ye the cornet in Gibeah, and the trumpet in Ramah: cry aloud at Beth-aven, after thee, O Benjamin.

9 Ephraim shall be desolate in the day of rebuke: among the tribes of Israel have I made known that which shall surely be.

10 The princes of Judah were like them that remove the bound: therefore I will pour out my wrath upon them like water.

11 Ephraim is oppressed and broken in judgment, because he willingly walked after the commandment.

12 Therefore will I be unto Ephraim as a moth, and to the house of Judah as rottenness.

13 When Ephraim saw his sickness, and Judah saw his wound, then went Ephraim to the Assyrian, and sent to king Jareb: yet could he not heal you, nor cure you of your wound.

14 For I will be unto Ephraim as a lion, and as a young lion to the house of Judah: I, even I, will tear and go away; I will take away, and none shall rescue him.

15 I will go and return to my place, till they acknowledge their offense, and seek my face: in their affliction they will seek me early.

CHAPTER 6

1 Come, and let us return unto the Lord: for he hath torn, and he will heal us; he hath smitten, and he will bind us up.

2 After two days will he revive us: in the third day he will raise us up, and we shall live in his sight.

3 Then shall we know, if we follow on to know the Lord: his going forth is prepared as the morning; and he shall come unto us as the rain, as the latter and former rain unto the earth.

4 O Ephraim, what shall I do unto thee? O Judah, what shall I do unto thee? for your goodness is as a morning cloud, and as the early dew it goeth away.

5 Therefore have I hewed them by the prophets; I have slain them by the words of my mouth: and thy judgments are as the light that goeth forth.

6 For I desired mercy, and not sacrifice; and the knowledge of God more than burnt offerings.

7 But they like men have transgressed the covenant: there have they dealt treacherously against me.

8 Gilead is a city of them that work iniquity, and is polluted with blood.

9 And as troops of robbers wait for a man, so the company of priests murder in the way by consent: for they commit lewdness.

10 I have seen a horrible thing in the house of Israel: there is the whoredom of Ephraim, Israel is defiled.

11 Also, O Judah, he hath set a harvest for thee, when I returned the captivity of my people.

CHAPTER 7

1 When I would have healed Israel, then the iniquity of Ephraim was discovered, and the wickedness of Samaria: for they commit falsehood; and the thief cometh in, and the troop of robbers spoileth without.

2 And they consider not in their hearts that I remember all their wickedness: now their own doings have beset them about; they are before my face.

3 They make the king glad with their wickedness, and the princes with their lies.

4 They are all adulterers, as an oven heated by the baker, who ceaseth from raising after he hath kneaded the dough, until it be leavened.

5 In the day of our king, the princes have made him sick with bottles of wine; he stretched out his hand with scorners.

6 For they have made ready their heart like an oven, while they lie in wait: their baker sleepeth all the night; in the morning it burneth as a flaming fire.

7 They are all hot as an oven, and have devoured their judges; all their kings are fallen: there is none among them that calleth unto me.

8 Ephraim, he hath mixed himself among the people; Ephraim is a cake not turned.

9 Strangers have devoured his strength, and he knoweth it not: yea, gray hairs are here and there upon him, yet he knoweth not.

10 And the pride of Israel testifieth to his face: and they do not return to the Lord their God, nor seek him for all this.

11 Ephraim also is like a silly dove without heart: they call to Egypt, they go to Assyria.

12 When they shall go, I will spread my net upon them; I will bring them down as the fowls of the heaven; I will chastise them, as their congregation hath heard.

13 Woe unto them! for they have fled from me: destruction unto them! because they have transgressed against me: though I have redeemed them, yet they have spoken lies against me.

14 And they have not cried unto me with their heart, when they howled upon their beds: they assemble themselves for corn and wine, and they rebel against me.

15 Though I have bound and strengthened their arms, yet do they imagine mischief against me.

16 They return, but not to the Most High: they are like a deceitful bow: their princes shall fall by the sword for the rage of their tongue: this shall be their derision in the land of Egypt.

CHAPTER 8

1 Set the trumpet to thy mouth. He shall come as an eagle against the house of the Lord, because they have transgressed my covenant, and trespassed against my law.

2 Israel shall cry unto me, My God, we know thee.

3 Israel hath cast off the thing that is good: the enemy shall pursue him.

4 They have set up kings, but not by me: they have made princes, and I knew it not: of their silver and their gold have they made them idols, that they may be cut off.

5 Thy calf, O Samaria, hath cast thee off; mine anger is kindled against them: how long will it be ere they attain to innocency?

6 For from Israel was it also: the workman made it; therefore it is not God: but the calf of Samaria shall be broken in pieces.

7 For they have sown the wind, and they shall reap the whirlwind: it hath no stalk: the bud shall yield no meal: if so be it yield, the strangers shall swallow it up.

8 Israel is swallowed up: now shall they be among the Gentiles as a vessel wherein is no pleasure.

9 For they are gone up to Assyria, a wild ass alone by himself: Ephraim hath hired lovers.

10 Yea, though they have hired among the nations, now will I gather them, and they shall sorrow a little for the burden of the king of princes.

11 Because Ephraim hath made many altars to sin, altars shall be unto him to sin.

12 I have written to him the great things of my law, but they were counted as a strange thing.

13 They sacrifice flesh for the sacrifices of mine offerings, and eat it: but the Lord accepteth them not; now will he remember their iniquity, and visit their sins: they shall return to Egypt.

14 For Israel hath forgotten his Maker, and buildeth temples; and Judah hath multiplied fenced cities: but I will send a fire upon his cities, and it shall devour the palaces thereof.

CHAPTER 9

1 Rejoice not, O Israel, for joy, as other people: for thou hast gone a whoring from thy God, thou hast loved a reward upon every cornfloor.

2 The floor and the winepress shall not feed them, and the new wine shall fail in her.

3 They shall not dwell in the Lord's land; but Ephraim shall return to Egypt, and they shall eat unclean things in Assyria.

4 They shall not offer wine offerings to the Lord, neither shall they be pleasing unto him: their sacrifices shall be unto them as the bread of mourners; all that eat thereof shall be polluted: for their bread for their soul shall not come into the house of the Lord.

5 What will ye do in the solemn day, and in the day of the feast of the Lord?

6 For, lo, they are gone because of destruction; Egypt shall gather them up, Memphis shall bury them: the pleasant places for their silver, nettles shall possess them: thorns shall be in their tabernacles.

7 The days of visitation are come, the days of recompense are come; Israel shall know it: the prophet is a fool, the spiritual man is mad, for the multitude of thine iniquity, and the great hatred.

8 The watchman of Ephraim was with my God: but the prophet is a snare of a fowler in all his ways, and hatred in the house of his God.

9 They have deeply corrupted themselves, as in the days of Gibeah: therefore he will remember their iniquity, he will visit their sins.

10 I found Israel like grapes in the wilderness; I saw your fathers as the first ripe in the fig tree at her first time: but they went to Baal-peor, and separated themselves unto that shame; and their abominations were according as they loved.

11 As for Ephraim, their glory shall fly away like a bird, from the birth, and from the womb, and from the conception.

12 Though they bring up their children, yet will I bereave them, that there shall not be a man left: yea, woe also to them when I depart from them!

13 Ephraim, as I saw Tyrus, is planted in a pleasant place: but Ephraim shall bring forth his children to the murderer.

HOSEA

14 Give them, O Lord: what wilt thou give? give them a miscarrying womb and dry breasts.

15 All their wickedness is in Gilgal: for there I hated them: for the wickedness of their doings I will drive them out of mine house, I will love them no more: all their princes are revolters.

16 Ephraim is smitten, their root is dried up, they shall bear no fruit: yea, though they bring forth, yet will I slay even the beloved fruit of their womb.

17 My God will cast them away, because they did not hearken unto him: and they shall be wanderers among the nations.

CHAPTER 10

1 Israel is an empty vine, he bringeth forth fruit unto himself: according to the multitude of his fruit he hath increased the altars; according to the goodness of his land they have made goodly images.

2 Their heart is divided; now shall they be found faulty: he shall break down their altars, he shall spoil their images.

3 For now they shall say, We have no king, because we feared not the Lord; what then should a king do to us?

4 They have spoken words, swearing falsely in making a covenant: thus judgment springeth up as hemlock in the furrows of the field.

5 The inhabitants of Samaria shall fear because of the calves of Beth-aven: for the people thereof shall mourn over it, and the priests thereof that rejoiced on it, for the glory thereof, because it is departed from it.

6 It shall be also carried unto Assyria for a present to king Jareb: Ephraim shall receive shame, and Israel shall be ashamed of his own counsel.

7 As for Samaria, her king is cut off as the foam upon the water.

8 The high places also of Aven, the sin of Israel, shall be destroyed: the thorn and thistle shall come up on their altars; and they shall say to the mountains, Cover us; and to the hills, Fall on us.

9 O Israel, thou hast sinned from the days of Gibeah: there they stood: the battle in Gibeah against the children of iniquity did not overtake them.

10 It is my desire that I should chastise them; and the people shall be gathered against them, when they shall bind themselves in their two furrows.

11 And Ephraim is as a heifer that is taught, and loveth to tread out the corn; but I passed over upon her fair neck: I will make Ephraim to ride; Judah shall plow, and Jacob shall break his clods.

12 Sow to yourselves in righteousness, reap in mercy; break up your fallow ground: for it is time to seek the Lord, till he come and rain righteousness upon you.

13 Ye have plowed wickedness, ye have reaped iniquity; ye have eaten the fruit of lies: because thou didst trust in thy way, in the multitude of thy mighty men.

14 Therefore shall a tumult arise among thy people, and all thy fortresses shall be spoiled, as Shalman spoiled Beth-arbel in the day of battle: the mother was dashed in pieces upon her children.

15 So shall Bethel do unto you because of your great wickedness: in a morning shall the king of Israel utterly be cut off.

CHAPTER 11

1 When Israel was a child, then I loved him, and called my son out of Egypt.

2 As they called them, so they went from them: they sacrificed unto Baalim, and burned incense to graven images.

3 I taught Ephraim also to go, taking them by their arms; but they knew not that I healed them.

4 I drew them with cords of a man, with bands of love: and I was to them as they that take off the yoke on their jaws, and I laid meat unto them.

5 He shall not return into the land of Egypt, but the Assyrian shall be his king, because they refused to return.

6 And the sword shall abide on his cities, and shall consume his branches, and devour them, because of their own counsels.

7 And my people are bent to backsliding from me: though they called them to the Most High, none at all would exalt him.

8 How shall I give thee up, Ephraim? how shall I deliver thee, Israel? how shall I make thee as Admah? how shall I set thee as Zeboim? mine heart is turned within me, my repentings are kindled together.

9 I will not execute the fierceness of mine anger, I will not return to destroy Ephraim: for I am God, and not man; the Holy One in the midst of thee: and I will not enter into the city.

10 They shall walk after the Lord: he shall roar like a lion: when he shall roar, then the children shall tremble from the west.

11 They shall tremble as a bird out of Egypt, and as a dove out of the land of Assyria: and I will place them in their houses, saith the Lord.

12 Ephraim compasseth me about with lies, and the house of Israel with deceit: but Judah yet ruleth with God, and is faithful with the saints.

CHAPTER 12

1 Ephraim feedeth on wind, and followeth after the east wind: he daily increaseth lies and desolation: and they do make a covenant with the Assyrians, and oil is carried into Egypt.

2 The Lord hath also a controversy with Judah, and will punish Jacob according to his ways; according to his doings will he recompense him.

3 He took his brother by the heel in the womb, and by his strength he had power with God:

4 Yea, he had power over the angel, and prevailed: he wept, and made supplication unto him: he found him in Bethel, and there he spake with us;

5 Even the Lord God of hosts; the Lord is his memorial.

6 Therefore turn thou to thy God: keep mercy and judgment, and wait on thy God continually.

7 He is a merchant, the balances of deceit are in his hand: he loveth to oppress.

8 And Ephraim said, Yet I am become rich, I have found me out substance: in all my labors they shall find none iniquity in me that were sin.

9 And I that am the Lord thy God from the land of Egypt will yet make thee to dwell in tabernacles, as in the days of the solemn feast.

10 I have also spoken by the prophets, and I have multiplied visions, and used similitudes, by the ministry of the prophets.

11 Is there iniquity in Gilead? surely they are vanity: they sacrifice bullocks in Gilgal; yea, their altars are as heaps in the furrows of the fields.

12 And Jacob fled into the country of Syria, and Israel served for a wife, and for a wife he kept sheep.

13 And by a prophet the Lord brought Israel out of Egypt, and by a prophet was he preserved.

14 Ephraim provoked him to anger most bitterly: therefore shall he leave his blood upon him, and his reproach shall his Lord return unto him.

CHAPTER 13

1 When Ephraim spake trembling, he exalted himself in Israel; but when he offended in Baal, he died.

2 And now they sin more and more and have made them molten images of their silver, and idols according to their own understanding, all of it the

work of the craftsmen: they say of
them, Let the men that sacrifice kiss
the calves.

3 Therefore they shall be as the
morning cloud, and as the early dew
that passeth away, as the chaff that is
driven with the whirlwind out of the
floor, and as the smoke out of the
chimney.

4 Yet I am the Lord thy God from
the land of Egypt, and thou shalt
know no god but me: for there is no
saviour beside me.

5 I did know thee in the wilderness, in the land of great drought.

6 According to their pasture, so
were they filled; they were filled, and
their heart was exalted; therefore
have they forgotten me.

7 Therefore I will be unto them as
a lion: as a leopard by the way will
I observe them:

8 I will meet them as a bear that
is bereaved of her whelps, and will
rend the caul of their heart, and there
will I devour them like a lion: the
wild beast shall tear them.

9 O Israel, thou hast destroyed
thyself; but in me is thine help.

10 I will be thy king: where is any
other that may save thee in all thy
cities? and thy judges of whom thou
saidst, Give me a king and princes?

11 I gave thee a king in mine anger, and took him away in my wrath.

12 The iniquity of Ephraim is
bound up; his sin is hid.

13 The sorrows of a travailing
woman shall come upon him: he is
an unwise son; for he should not stay
long in the place of the breaking forth
of children.

14 I shall ransom them from the
power of the grave; I will redeem
them from death: O death, I will be
thy plagues; O grave, I will be thy
destruction: repentance shall be hid
from mine eyes.

15 Though he be fruitful among
his brethren, an east wind shall come,
the wind of the Lord shall come up
from the wilderness, and his spring
shall become dry, and his fountain
shall be dried up: he shall spoil the
treasure of all pleasant vessels.

16 Samaria shall become desolate;
for she hath rebelled against her
God: they shall fall by the sword:
their infants shall be dashed in pieces,
and their women with child shall be
ripped up.

CHAPTER 14

1 O Israel, return unto the Lord
thy God; for thou hast fallen by
thine iniquity.

2 Take with you words, and turn
to the Lord: say unto him, Take away
all iniquity, and receive us graciously:
so will we render the calves of our
lips.

3 Asshur shall not save us; we will
not ride upon horses: neither will we
say any more to the work of our
hands, Ye are our gods: for in thee
the fatherless findeth mercy.

4 I will heal their backsliding, I
will love them freely: for mine anger
is turned away from him.

5 I will be as the dew unto Israel:
he shall grow as the lily, and cast
forth his roots as Lebanon.

6 His branches shall spread, and
his beauty shall be as the olive tree,
and his smell as Lebanon.

7 They that dwell under his shadow
shall return; they shall revive as the
corn, and grow as the vine: the
scent thereof shall be as the wine of
Lebanon.

8 Ephraim shall say, What have I
to do any more with idols? I have
heard him, and observed him: I am
like a green fir tree. From me is thy
fruit found.

9 Who is wise, and he shall understand these things? prudent, and he
shall know them? for the ways of the
Lord are right, and the just shall walk
in them: but the transgressors shall
fall therein.

HOSEA—SPIRITUAL ADULTERY

A. THE PROPHET AND HIS TIMES (HOSEA 1:1)

I. *Dates*. The prophet dates his prophesying by giving the names of four kings of Judah, and one king of Israel. A tabulation of these will enable us to determine approximately the length of his prophesying and the history of their reigns reveals the condition of the times.

Jeroboam, King of Israel,	41 years (15 years with Uzziah).
Uzziah, King of Judah,	52 years (37 after Jeroboam's death).
Jotham, King of Judah,	16 years
Ahaz, King of Judah,	16 years
Hezekiah, King of Judah	29 years

This reveals a remarkable length of prophetic utterance. Hosea's voice was heard in reigns that covered no less a period than 138 years. How long he actually prophesied we have no means of knowing, but it could not have been less than about seventy years.

Of Hosea himself we know nothing, save that he was the son of Beeri, and what we learn of his domestic life from the prophecy itself.

II. *Characteristics*. The period covered by the prophesying of Hosea was undoubtedly the darkest in the whole history of the kingdom of Israel. It embraced the latter part of the ninth and most of the eighth centuries before Christ. The only king of Israel to whom he refers is Jeroboam, who was the last king but one who was God-appointed.

God promised Jehu (II Kings 15:8) that four generations should occupy the throne. Jeroboam was the third, and his son, Zechariah, after an interregnum of twenty-two years, reigned six months. Then followed the most terrible condition of affairs. The political life was characterized by anarchy and misrule. Kings came to the throne over the murder of others. Zechariah was slain by Shallum; he was slain by Menahem; Pekiah, his son, was slain by Pekah, and he in turn was slain by Hoshea, the last king of Israel. These were soldiers, so that there existed during this time a military despotism.

Foreign alliances in the past (e.g., Baasha with Benhadad, King of Syria, and Ahab's marriage to Jezebel, daughter of the King of Tyre), and more recently (e.g., Menahem paying tribute to Pul, King of Assyria, and Pekah with Rezin) had involved the nation in inextricable confusion. They constantly endeavored to play these off against each other, and yet were under the oppression of all.

Religion: These alliances had brought the corruptions of Syrian and Phoenician idolatry. Through all these years there was continued the false worship set up by Jeroboam I. This consisted in a magnificent worship of God under the form of a calf. It was practically the deification of nature and, while at first it was intended to recognize the one God through a likeness, it led inevitably to the forgetfulness of God and all the evil results which always follow in the wake of nature worship.

The resulting conditions were the most revolting pollution; luxurious living, robbery, oppression, falsehood, adultery, murder; and accompanying these was the most violent intolerance of any form of rebuke.

The message of the prophet is to Israel in its imperfect state as the kingdom of the ten tribes. Israel is mentioned or addressed forty-four times in the prophecy. The influencing tribe was ever Ephraim, which was also the largest. The divine recognition of this is marked in the mention of Ephraim thirty-seven times and especially in 7:1 and 13:1. Judah is also always in view for warning, as is seen in the fifteen times she is mentioned.

B. THE ANALYSIS OF THE PROPHECY

I. The training of the prophet (chapters 1–3).

a. The prophet's domestic life and his national conscience (1:2 —2:1).

    1. The word of the Lord "at the first" (verse 2). This is the language of Hosea in after years. Looking back he understands that the impulse which has resulted in heart agony was also part of the divine method of teaching him.

    2. The marriage (verse 3).

3. The domestic life and his national conscience (verses
   4–9).
   (a) The birth of the children. There is no reason to be-
       lieve these were children of sin.
   (b) The prophet's inner life. (1) Hosea was so much in
       communion with God that He named the children.
       (2) In the light of that communion Hosea was ob-
       serving his own people.
   (c) The revelation of that communion concerning the
       nation in the naming of the children. (1) Jezreel—
       "The threatened judgment." (2) Lo-Ruhamah—
       "Mercy not obtained." (3) Lo-Ammi—"Cast out."
       "Not my people."
4. The vision of hope (1:10—2:1). Notice the seven "shalls"
   of verses 10, 11, and the triumphant announcement of 2:1.

b. The tragedy in the prophet's home, and its revelation of the
   sin of Israel as God feels it (2:2–23).
   1. The charge (verses 2–5). Hosea and Jehovah.
      (a) "She hath played the harlot." This is even worse than
          adultery (verse 5).
      (b) "The awful anger of wounded love" (verses 3, 4).
      (c) The suggestion of pity and mercy. "Let her put away"
          (verses 2, 3).
   2. The severity of love (verses 6–13). Jehovah only.
      (a) The program and its purpose (verses 6, 7). (1) The
          way hedged up. (2) The fruitless search for lovers.
          (3) The issue aimed at is her return.
      (b) Explanation of this program (verses 8–13). (1) The
          very gifts sought are from God. (2) These He will
          withdraw. (3) Then shall she know her shame.
   3. The tenderness of love (verses 14–23). Jehovah only.
      (a) The wilderness (verses 14, 15). (1) Allured to the
          wilderness. (2) Speak to her heart. (3) From thence
          vineyards. Achor—a door of hope.
      (b) The results. (1) She shall sing as in the days of her
          youth. (2) Ishi instead of Baali. (3) The new be-
          trothal forever. (4) A new meaning to Jezreel;
          Ruhamah instead of Lo-Ruhamah; Ammi instead of
          Lo-Ammi.

c. The love of God to Israel creating the tenderness of the
prophet towards Gomer, and thus reflectively teaching him
the tenderness of God (chapter 3).

1. The instruction of Jehovah (verse 1).
   (a) "Go . . . love . . . as the Lord." Exercise love in
   spite of all the sin—that is God's attitude to Israel.
   (b) Jehovah's love to Israel inspired Hosea's love toward
   Gomer.

2. Hosea's obedience (verses 2, 3).
   (a) "I bought her." The price was about the price of a
   slave, which in all probability she had become.
   (b) The covenant: (1) For her a time of seclusion,
   neither harlot nor wife. (2) For him also. "So will I
   also be toward thee."

3. The national interpretation.
   (a) Israel's time of penance deprived them of the exercise
   of both the false and the true relationship.
   (b) The ultimate issue—Israel's return to all the honors
   and blessings of union with God.

Summary of the Training. Out of his own heart agony Hosea
learned the nature of the sin of his people. They were playing the
harlot, spending God's gifts in lewd traffic with other lovers. Out
of that agony he has learned how God suffers over the sin of His
people, because of His undying love. Out of God's love Hosea's
new care for Gomer was born, and in the method God ordained for
him with her, he discovered God's method with Israel. Out of all
this process of pain, there came full confidence in the ultimate victory of love. Thus equipped he delivers his messages and all
through them will sound these deep notes of Sin, Love, Hope.

II. The teaching of the prophet* (chapters 4—14).

a. The first cycle of the prophecy. Pollution and its cause (4:1—
6:3).

---

* In any attempt to analyze and tabulate the teaching contained in these
eleven chapters, it must be remembered that they can by no means be con-
sidered as verbatim reports of the prophet's message. They are rather the
gathering up of the notes or leading ideas in that long period of preaching.
This makes it difficult to analyze or tabulate. The basis on which the attempt
is now made is not that of the periods covered, but that of the subject matter.

1. The general charge (4:1-3).
    (a) Israel is summoned to attend and hear the word of the Lord, because He has a controversy with the inhabitants of the land.
    (b) The charge. (1) Negative. No truth; no mercy; no knowledge of God. (2) Positive. Nought but swearing and breaking faith, killing, stealing, committing adultery. An awful picture! Mark the antithesis; note the sequence.
    (c) The result. (1) The mourning land (uncultivated). (2) The languishing people. (3) Man's dominion lost over beasts, fowls, fishes.
2. The cause declared; and the results described (4:4-19).
    (a) The cause. The pollution of the priests (verses 4-10).
    (b) The result. The pollution of the people (verses 11-19).
3. Special message to priests, people and king (chapter 5).
    (a) The summons and the charge (verses 1-7). (1) Priests and king as leaders and responsible. (2) "I know" (verses 3-7).
    (b) The judgment (verses 8-15). (1) The proclamation. (2) Results of judgment. (3) Methods of judgment—progressive—moth and rottenness; young lion; withdrawal.
4. The plaintive plea of the prophet (7:1-3).
    (a) The message in its local application. (1) A call to return based upon the certainty of the divine pity. (2) The great certainty of prosperity there is in return to Him.
    (b) The Messianic application.
b. The second cycle of the prophecy. Pollution and its punishment (6:4—10:15).
    1. The case stated (6:4—7:16).
        (a) The Divine attitude (6:4-6).
        (b) The human response (6:7-11).
        (c) The true state of affairs (chapter 7). (1) The divine desire to heal frustrated by discovery of pollution and by ignoring God. (2) Pollution is everywhere. (3) Ephraim. (4) The utter folly of the people.

2. The judgment pronounced (chapters 8, 9).
   (a) The trumpet to the mouth (chapter 8). Five blasts—transgression, rebellion, idolatry, alliances, altars of sin.
   (b) The whirlwind (chapter 9). (1) The death of joy. (2) Exile. (3) Cessation of prophecy. (4) The nemesis of fornication. (5) Cast out.
3. Recapitulation and appeal (chapter 10).
   (a) The whole case (verses 1, 2).
   (b) The lament and its reason (verses 3–8).
   (c) Sin and chastisement (verses 9–11).
   (d) The appeal of severity (verses 12–15).

c. The third cycle of the prophecy. The love of Jehovah (chapters 11—14).

1. The message of Jehovah with the prophet's interpolations (chapters 11—13).

This section contains the declaration of the attitude of Jehovah towards His sinning people, and is the speech of Jehovah Himself for the most part. He sums up, and in so doing declares His sense of the awfulness of the sin, pronouncing His righteous judgments, yet through all, the dominant notes are those of His love, and the ultimate victory of that love over sin and judgment. Thrice the prophet interpolates words of his own. The section is divided by taking the words of Jehovah in sequence, and then the interpolations of the prophet.

   (a) The message of Jehovah (11:1–12; 12:1, 7–11; 13:2–14). (1) The present in the light of past love (11:1–11). (2) The present in the light of present love (11:12; 12:1, 7–10). (3) The present in the light of the future love (12:11; 13:2–14).
   (b) The prophet's interpolations (12:2–6, 12; 13:1, 15, 16). (1) The prophet's sense of Jehovah's controversy with Judah, and his just dealings with Jacob (12:2). (2) Reminiscent of Jacob's history, with a deduction and an appeal (12:3–6). (3) The progress of Israel to death (12:12—13:1). (4) The doom (13:15, 16).

These interpolations tell the history of Israel, indicate his relation to Jehovah, and pronounce judgment. They form a remarkable obligato accompaniment to the majestic love song of Jehovah, and form a contrasting introduction to the final message of the prophet.

    2.   The final call of the prophet, with the promise of Jehovah (chapter 14).

        (a) The call (14:1–3). (1) Return, for thou hast fallen by iniquity. (2) The method suggested.

        (b) The answer of Jehovah (14:4–7). (1) Restoration. (2) Renewal. (3) Reinstatement. Ephraim's speech: What have I to do any more with idols? Him I have answered and will regard. I am like a green fir-tree.

Epilogue (14:9). The prophet's addendum, an application for all time.

The Message of Hosea

This analysis reveals the message that the prophet delivered to his age; it gathers around three words, <u>Sin, Judgment and Love.</u> While dealing incidentally and definitely with different forms of *sin,* the prophet saw and declared its essential nature. The people chosen of God to be His own, a people upon whom He had lavished His love, had turned their backs upon Him and were spending the very gifts of His love in lewdness until they had actually committed the awful sins of adultery and harlotry. What this meant to God, Hosea learned by the horrible tragedy in his own home and in his heart, and with fierce and hot anger he denounces priests, kings, princes, judges, and people alike.

As to *judgment* the prophet was ever careful to emphasize the fact that judgment is the necessary result of sin, and he declares the judgments in all their awful force and completeness, and he showed clearly that for such sin man had no right to entertain the faintest hope of pardon, and should only look to the carrying out of the sentence to the last item. Notwithstanding the greatest fact in his message; namely, that of love's ultimate triumph, he clearly discerned and emphatically declared that the triumph of love was postponed and that the generation which he addressed would be swept away in the flood of judgment.

But the great note of Hosea's message is the *love* note. In the midst of his own overwhelming sorrow, God had called him to such attitude and action towards Gomer, his sinning wife, as must have astonished him beyond measure, for in the heart of man under such circumstances there is no thought of restoration for the degraded one; yet with tender severity and severe tenderness, in obedience to the Word of God, he found Gomer and ultimately restored her to her forfeited place. Out of that experience he learned the deepest secret of the heart of God, that of its mighty, its unceasing love, and therefore this prophecy, so tragic and awful in its picture of human sin and divine judgment, thrills to the tireless music of a psalm, and the dominant note is that of love, so amazing that in its presence none can but be astonished and subdued.

C. The Permanent Message

I. *Stated.* Leaving all the local coloring, which has faded with the passing of the centuries, there yet remain essential principles which have a present application, and which gather around the same words. The prophecy of Hosea has to this age a great message about sin, about judgment, and about love. The most heinous and damnable sin of which man is capable is that of infidelity to love. This is the sin of all such as have been brought into right relationship with God, and then, violating love's covenant, have committed spiritual adultery with His enemies. Compared with a sin like that, the animalism, the brutality and the corruption of heathen nations is as nothing. Hosea's message concerning sin leaves no alternative but the conclusion that it were better to have lived life out in darkness with no knowledge of God than, having had the light, to turn back to the things from which the divine love had separated.

Judgment. Such sinning generates the form of judgment that follows it. Judgement is not a stroke of God inflicted upon a man as apart from a man's sin. It is the outworking of the sin itself. The pathway of infidelity can lead nowhere save to the unutterable darkness of pollution. No surface repentance which is a mere device to escape punishment can be accepted with God. The penalties of apostasy are as irrevocable as are the laws of purity.

Love. Yet the love song of Jehovah continues and even though the pathway of love's triumph lies through suffering, of which no man can ever know the measure, and the cost of the restoration of the unfaithful lover be that of the bearing of the judgment by the faithful lover, still love moves right onward to the goal, and sings the song of the victory that is to be.

These are the permanent notes of the message. To emphasize either of them apart from the others is to minimize the value of the whole. Let each be pondered and, so far as we are called to speak the message of God to our age, let the notes be clear and unmixed.

II. *Applied.* The application of this prophetic message to the present age can only fairly be made as a general outlook is taken upon Christendom. I have no right to make an application of this message to churches or to a local church. As the message was not to a tribe, but to the nation, one tribe only being referred to perpetually, because it was the leading tribe and the most guilty sinner, so the permanent message can only be applied to the whole of Christendom. Whatever message it may contain for the Catholic Church or for a local church does not come within the scope of these studies.

What is the message? *Sin.* The causes of the Church's failure are those of the failure of Israel of old. Spiritual adultery is evidenced by the paganism which has become admixtured with the things of God. Witness the Roman and the Greek Churches and all in other communities which are of the habit and spirit of these—ritualism, formalism, and self-centered satisfaction that will excommunicate those who differ from them. Don't you be too angry with the Pope in Rome as long as you are a pope yourself. The harlotry of worldliness is in all the churches at this present moment. Thousands who name the name of Christ are taking possessions which have been bestowed upon God and are spending them in the pursuit of worldly ambitions and pleasures. Blood-bought souls are at this hour inflaming themselves with carnality under every green tree. Through these things the testimony which should be borne to other nations is silenced, and the name of God is being profaned among the heathen.

What about *judgment?* The judgment of God is already upon the guilty people on whom His love is set. The judgment of the moth and the judgment of the rottenness is everywhere. It is manifested in the weakness for all divine purposes of the hosts of God. It is enough to sadden the heart, the fact that the Church of Christ as a whole hardly seems able to speak any authoritative word to the councils of the nations, that the Church of Jesus Christ is mourning the dearth of conversions, is discussing in her religious papers and is wondering at the depletion of her theological schools. Like Ephraim, she turns to Egypt and Assyria for help, and is thereby minished and laid low. Let us remember solemnly that beyond the moth and the rottenness is the method of the "young lion," and beyond the young lion is the withdrawal of Jehovah. It is just as certain that God will cast off the Church itself as that He cast off Israel, unless the Church fulfills its function. I am not talking about eternal purposes now. Israel will yet be restored and God will yet carry out His purpose in the great Church, but unless we repent in dust and ashes of our harlotry and our adultery and our worldliness, we will be abandoned from service. The solemn word will come to all of us. "No more in the stewardship."

Love. And yet over all the failure, heartbreaking and desolating though it be, there still sounds the music of Jehovah's love, and the assurance remains that He has not exhausted His methods, but another crisis is coming, and that beyond that and through it He will realize His triumph. "I will redeem; I will bring back." At the coming of Christ love will triumph through judgment, and at last over judgment. The triumph is certain because Jehovah is God and not man. May God grant that we as Christian workers catch the notes of Hosea's great message, sin, judgment and love, and laying emphasis upon them all, gather the perfect harmony of the message and tell it to the age in which we live.

CHAPTER 2

JOEL

CHAPTER 1

1 The word of the Lord that came to Joel the son of Pethuel.

2 Hear this, ye old men, and give ear, all ye inhabitants of the land. Hath this been in your days, or even in the days of your fathers?

3 Tell ye your children of it, and let your children tell their children, and their children another generation.

4 That which the palmerworm hath left hath the locust eaten; and that which the locust hath left hath the cankerworm eaten; and that which the cankerworm hath left hath the caterpillar eaten.

5 Awake, ye drunkards, and weep; and howl, all ye drinkers of wine, because of the new wine; for it is cut off from your mouth.

6 For a nation is come up upon my land, strong, and without number, whose teeth are the teeth of a lion, and he hath the cheek teeth of a great lion.

7 He hath laid my vine waste, and barked my fig tree: he hath made it clean bare, and cast it away; the branches thereof are made white.

8 Lament like a virgin girded with sackcloth for the husband of her youth.

9 The meat offering and the drink offering is cut off from the house of the Lord; the priests, the Lord's ministers, mourn.

10 The field is wasted, the land mourneth; for the corn is wasted: the new wine is dried up, the oil languisheth.

11 Be ye ashamed, O ye husbandmen; howl, O ye vinedressers, for the wheat and for the barley; because the harvest of the field is perished.

12 The vine is dried up, and the fig tree languisheth; the pomegranate tree, the palm tree also, and the apple tree, even all the trees of the field, are withered: because joy is withered away from the sons of men.

13 Gird yourselves, and lament, ye priests: howl, ye ministers of the altar: come, lie all night in sackcloth, ye ministers of my God: for the meat offering and the drink offering is withholden from the house of your God.

14 Sanctify ye a fast, call a solemn assembly, gather the elders and all the inhabitants of the land into the house of the Lord your God, and cry unto the Lord,

15 Alas for the day! for the day of the Lord is at hand, and as a destruction from the Almighty shall it come.

16 Is not the meat cut off before our eyes, yea, joy and gladness from the house of our God?

17 The seed is rotten under their clods, the garners are laid desolate, the barns are broken down; for the corn is withered.

18 How do the beasts groan! the herds of cattle are perplexed, because they have no pasture; yea, the flocks of sheep are made desolate.

19 O Lord, to thee will I cry: for the fire hath devoured the pastures of the wilderness, and the flame hath burned all the trees of the field.

20 The beasts of the field cry also unto thee: for the rivers of water are dried up, and the fire hath devoured the pastures of the wilderness.

CHAPTER 2

1 Blow ye the trumpet in Zion, and sound an alarm in my holy mountain: let all the inhabitants of the land tremble: for the day of the Lord cometh, for it is nigh at hand;

2 A day of darkness and of gloominess, a day of clouds and of thick darkness, as the morning spread upon the mountains: a great people and a strong; there hath not been ever the like, neither shall be any more after it, even to the years of many generations.

3 A fire devoureth before them; and behind them a flame burneth: the land is as the garden of Eden before them, and behind them a desolate wilderness; yea, and nothing shall escape them.

4 The appearance of them is as the appearance of horses; and as horsemen, so shall they run.

5 Like the noise of chariots on the tops of mountains shall they leap, like the noise of a flame of fire that devoureth the stubble, as a strong people set in battle array.

6 Before their face the people shall be much pained: all faces shall gather blackness.

7 They shall run like mighty men; they shall climb the wall like men of war; and they shall march every one on his ways, and they shall not break their ranks:

8 Neither shall one thrust another; they shall walk every one in his path: and when they fall upon the sword, they shall not be wounded.

9 They shall run to and fro in the city; they shall run upon the wall, they shall climb up upon the houses; they shall enter in at the windows like a thief.

10 The earth shall quake before them; the heavens shall tremble: the sun and the moon shall be dark, and the stars shall withdraw their shining:

11 And the Lord shall utter his voice before his army: for his camp is very great: for he is strong that executeth his word: for the day of of the Lord is great and very terrible; and who can abide it?

12 Therefore also now, saith the Lord, turn ye even to me with all your heart, and with fasting, and with weeping, and with mourning:

13 And rend your heart, and not your garments, and turn unto the Lord your God: for he is gracious and merciful, slow to anger, and of great kindness, and repenteth him of the evil.

14 Who knoweth if he will return and repent, and leave a blessing behind him; even a meat offering and a drink offering unto the Lord your God?

15 Blow the trumpet in Zion, sanctify a fast, call a solemn assembly:

16 Gather the people, sanctify the congregation, assemble the elders, gather the children, and those that suck the breasts: let the bridegroom go forth of his chamber, and the bride out of her closet.

17 Let the priests, the ministers of the Lord, weep between the porch and the altar, and let them say, Spare thy people, O Lord, and give not thine heritage to reproach, that the heathen should rule over them:

wheretore should they say among the people, Where is their God?

18 Then will the Lord be jealous for his land, and pity his people.

19 Yea, the Lord will answer and say unto his people, Behold, I will send you corn, and wine, and oil, and ye shall be satisfied therewith: and I will no more make you a reproach among the heathen:

20 But I will remove far off from you the northern army, and will drive him into a land barren and desolate, with his face toward the east sea, and his hinder part toward the utmost sea, and his stink shall come up, and his ill savor shall come up, because he hath done great things.

21 Fear not, O land; be glad and rejoice: for the Lord will do great things.

22 Be not afraid, ye beasts of the field: for the pastures of the wilderness do spring, for the tree beareth her fruit, the fig tree and the vine do yield their strength.

23 Be glad then, ye children of Zion, and rejoice in the Lord your God: for he hath given you the former rain moderately, and he will cause to come down for you the rain, the former rain, and the latter rain in the first month.

24 And the floors shall be full of wheat, and the vats shall overflow with wine and oil.

25 And I will restore to you the years that the locust hath eaten, the cankerworm, and the caterpillar, and the palmerworm, my great army which I sent among you.

26 And ye shall eat in plenty, and be satisfied, and praise the name of the Lord your God, that hath dealt wondrously with you: and my people shall never be ashamed.

27 And ye shall know that I am in the midst of Israel, and that I am the Lord your God, and none else: and my people shall never be ashamed.

28 And it shall come to pass afterward, that I will pour out my Spirit upon all flesh; and your sons and your daughters shall prophesy, your old men shall dream dreams, your young men shall see visions:

29 And also upon the servants and upon the handmaids in those days will I pour out my Spirit.

30 And I will show wonders in the heavens and in the earth, blood, and fire, and pillars of smoke.

31 The sun shall be turned into darkness, and the moon into blood, before the great and the terrible day of the Lord come.

32 And it shall come to pass, that whosoever shall call on the name of the Lord shall be delivered: for in mount Zion and in Jerusalem shall be deliverance, as the Lord hath said, and in the remnant whom the Lord shall call.

CHAPTER 3

1 For, behold, in those days, and in that time, when I shall bring again the captivity of Judah and Jerusalem,

2 I will also gather all nations, and will bring them down into the valley of Jehoshaphat, and will plead with them there for my people and for my heritage Israel, whom they have scattered among the nations, and parted my land.

3 And they have cast lots for my people; and have given a boy for a harlot, and sold a girl for wine, that they might drink.

4 Yea, and what have ye to do with me, O Tyre, and Zidon, and all the coasts of Palestine? will ye render me a recompense? and if ye recompense me, swiftly and speedily will I return your recompense upon your own head;

5 Because ye have taken my silver and my gold, and have carried into your temples my goodly pleasant things:

6 The children also of Judah and the children of Jerusalem have ye

sold unto the Grecians, that ye might remove them far from their border.

7 Behold, I will raise them out of the place whither ye have sold them, and will return your recompense upon your own head:

8 And I will sell your sons and your daughters into the hand of the children of Judah, and they shall sell them to the Sabeans, to a people far off: for the Lord hath spoken it.

9 Proclaim ye this among the Gentiles; Prepare war, wake up the mighty men, let all the men of war draw near; let them come up:

10 Beat your plowshares into swords, and your pruning hooks into spears: let the weak say, I am strong.

11 Assemble yourselves, and come, all ye heathen, and gather yourselves together round about: thither cause thy mighty ones to come down, O Lord.

12 Let the heathen be wakened, and come up to the valley of Jehoshaphat: for there will I sit to judge all the heathen round about.

13 Put ye in the sickle, for the harvest is ripe: come, get you down; for the press is full, the vats overflow; for their wickedness is great.

14 Multitudes, multitudes in the valley of decision: for the day of the Lord is near in the valley of decision.

15 The sun and the moon shall be darkened, and the stars shall withdraw their shining.

16 The Lord also shall roar out of Zion, and utter his voice from Jerusalem; and the heavens and the earth shall shake: but the Lord will be the hope of his people, and the strength of the children of Israel.

17 So shall ye know that I am the Lord your God dwelling in Zion, my holy mountain: then shall Jerusalem be holy, and there shall no strangers pass through her any more.

18 And it shall come to pass in that day, that the mountains shall drop down new wine, and the hills shall flow with milk, and all the rivers of Judah shall flow with waters, and a fountain shall come forth of the house of the Lord, and shall water the valley of Shittim.

19 Egypt shall be a desolation, and Edom shall be a desolate wilderness, for the violence against the children of Judah, because they have shed innocent blood in their land.

20 But Judah shall dwell for ever, and Jerusalem from generation to generation.

21 For I will cleanse their blood that I have not cleansed: for the Lord dwelleth in Zion.

JOEL—THE DAY OF JEHOVAH

A. THE PROPHET AND HIS TIMES

I. *Dates.* Nothing is known of the Prophet Joel save what may be gathered from the prophecy. The statement that he was the son of Pethuel is of no help, as we know no more of Pethuel than of Joel. Thus the date of the prophecy can only be gathered from internal evidence, and this is of so slender and doubtful a nature

as to leave the subject an open question. But there are certain
points of interest which help us to form an opinion:

a. The prophet makes no reference to Syrians, Assyrians, or
Chaldeans. He does mention Tyre, Sidon, and Philistia.

b. He makes no reference to idolatry or corruption, but he
speaks of the temple services as being maintained.

c. He is silent as to king or princes, but he refers to elders and
priest.

d. He had none of the scorn for the sacrifices which mark the
writings of other prophets. On the contrary he mourns that because
of the locust plague there are no offerings.

e. A large number of passages are found in the book, similar
to those in other prophetic writings.

These facts show that the prophecy could not have been uttered
during that period covered by the prophets from Amos to
Zechariah. They would find their explanation if Joel exercised his
gift in the early years of the reign of Joash, where on account of
his youth he had not as yet assumed the responsibilities of kingship.
They would be equally accounted for if the prophecy were post-
exilic.

II. *Characteristics*. Joel was especially a prophet to Judah, and
the burden of his message—which seems to be one remarkable
utterance rather than notes of a ministry covering a long period
like that of Hosea—is the "day of the Lord." A terrible locust
plague, which had devastated the entire country, was seen by the
prophet as a judgment of God; and this he declared, and announced the fact that it indicated a still severer judgment, which
could noly be averted by heart repentance.

This outlook and interpretation is made the basis of a larger
message. The prophet's mind is burdened with the fact of the
divine government, and the certainty that beyond all the failure
resulting from human administration, the time will come when
God will administer His own affairs. This period he speaks of
as the day of the Lord. He has a remarkable vision of the divine
program, which was to be ushered in by the outpouring of the
Holy Spirit. The burden is that of the day of the Lord, which
is declared to be a day of judgment and destruction, issuing in
a reign of order and the restoration of all things.

B. THE ANALYSIS OF THE PROPHECY

I. *Things present* (1:2—2:27).

a.   The locust plague and its first meaning (1:2–20).
　　1.   The call to contemplation (1:2–12).
　　　　(a) Address to the old men and all the inhabitants (verses 2–4).
　　　　(b) Address to the drunkards (verses 5–7).
　　　　(c) Address to worshipers (verses 8–10).
　　　　(d) Address to husbandmen and vinedressers (verses 11, 12).

Note. The prophet in this opening section calls attention to the completeness of the devastation, showing how it has affected all classes. Each section in differing figure emphasizes the utter destruction. The whole address shows all classes involved.

　　2.   The call to humiliation (verses 13–20).
　　　　(a) Beginning with the priests (verse 13). A solemn call and the reason.
　　　　(b) Including the people (verse 14). The summons and the injunction.
　　　　(c) Interpretation of plague, and reason of call to humiliation (verses 15–18).
　　　　(d) The prophet voices the cry of the assembled people (verses 19, 20).

Having thus dealt with the actual visitation, and its terrible devastation, and having called the people into the place of humiliation, the prophet rises to a higher level and interprets the present visitation as indicating a deeper and more terrible judgment imminent.

b.   The locust plague and its deeper teaching (2:1–27).
　　1.   The trumpet of alarm and the answer of God (verses 1–14).
　　　　(a) The trumpet of alarm (verses 1–11). (1) The announcement of the call and the reason (verse 1). (2) Descriptive (verses 2–10). Here, in one of the most graphic paragraphs, the prophet describes the locust plague. His mind is evidently on that which is past, but he uses it as symbolizing the swift, and

irresistible, and all-consuming character of the judgment of God, when it goes forth. (3) The directing
Jehovah (verse 11).

(b) The answer of God stated and enforced (verses 12–
14).

The prophet's conception of the repentance of God, and of the
blessing He leaves is that those receiving will have something to
offer Him. The prophet has thus indicated the imminence of
divine judgment, and the way by which it may probably be
averted. He now blows the second trumpet, which is in order to
call the people to the attitude so indicated.

2.   The trumpet of repentance and the answer of God (verses
15–27).

(a) The trumpet of repentance (verses 15–17). (1) The
assembling of the people, its solemn character and
constitution (verses 15, 16). (2) The exercise of the
assembly (verse 17).

(b) The answer of Jehovah (verses 18–27). In these
gracious answers of God to the repentant attitude
of the assembled people, the key is to be found by
comparing the close of verses 20 and 21. (1) Reference to the northern army. "He hath done great
things." (2) Reference to Jehovah. "Jehovah hath
done great things." These are the things of mercy.
Both the things of judgment and the things of mercy
are in the government of God, the first rendered necessary by the people's neglect of Him; the second
made possible by the people's return to Him. The
things of His mercy correct and abolish the things of
His judgment.

The prophet having indicated the judgment imminent, and
called the people to repentance, and having, moreover, declared
the merciful attitude of Jehovah toward such repentance, he has
now come to the end of his message as it has to do with the things
then present. He now moves on to a yet higher plane, and here is
granted to him a vision of that final day of the Lord, of which
the things present were but the shadow and the forecast. In the
next section, the prophet is dealing wholly with things to come.
The key word introducing it is "afterward." Some of the things

in this second section have now been fulfilled. Some are still in the future.

II. *Things to come* (2:28—3).

In looking toward the distant day of the Lord, the prophet saw an intervening period of an entirely different character. This he first describes, and then his message ends with a declaration concerning the day of the Lord, which was the real burden on his spirit.
a. The dispensation of the Spirit (2:28–32).
   1. Its initiation and characteristics (verses 28, 29).
   2. Signs of its ending and the coming of the day of the Lord (verses 30, 31).
   3. The deliverance from the horrors of that day (verse 32).
This is a perfect description of the pentecostal age in which we are now living, with a statement of the signs which presage its end, and a declaration of the day of deliverance from the horrors that immediately follow.
b. The day of the Lord (chapter 3).
   1. God's dealings with His ancient people (verses 1–8).
     (a) Restoration of Judah and Jerusalem (verse 1).
     (b) Finding of Israel (verses 2–8).
   2. God's judgment of the nations (verses 9–16).
   3. The restoration of Israel (verses 17–21).
The Lord dwelleth in Zion.

The Message of Joel

Joel's message to his time was preëminently one concerning the authoritative and overcoming government of God, but it was illumined all the way through by his consciousness of the divine grace.

The government of God. He declared the absolute supremacy of Jehovah, realizing in the plague of locusts, which gave rise to his message, the visitation of God. From this he deduced a warning of a yet more terrible visitation imminent. These messages led to a fuller vision and declaration of the ultimate realization of divine purposes through divine government. God is on the throne; that is the underlying thought.

The grace of God. How beautifully it was manifested! His message was equally one concerning the tenderness of Jehovah, for in response to repentance God was declared as ever averting judgment and acting in mercy; and even when the prophet dealt with the final acts of the divine government, he realized that a way of escape would be made for those who should call upon the name of the Lord. He realized, moreover, that the terrible scenes in the Valley of Jehoshaphat would end in the accomplishment of the purposes of Love.

Perhaps the most remarkable part of the prophecy to the man who uttered it, and the men who heard it, is the section which predicted the dispensation of the Spirit. Of all Old Testament predictions concerning the Spirit, there is none more concise or forceful than this of Joel.

C. The Permanent Message

I. *Stated.* The message of Joel is of value today in its declaration of principles and its revelation of a plan. The principles are those of the divine government and divine grace. The plan is that indicated by the postponement of judgment until after the accomplishment of the work of the Spirit. The present is not God's day of judgment; this is God's day of grace.

Take the *principles.* Jehovah occupies the throne. He in patience presides over the probation of man and presses into His service all kinds of armies and forces for the carrying out of His purpose. There is not an army that marches over the plains that is not held in check by God Almighty; there are no plagues of locusts sweeping over the country but they march at His command, and all that appears so chaotic, could we see it from the upper spaces, is rhythmic in its order as God is marching to order out of chaos. Oh, the comfort of it! That is Joel's message. It is always the day of the Lord. When devastation sweeps abroad, it is His day. When everything seems wrong, it is His day. This conviction in the heart makes a man say, The day of the Lord must come eventually when all that is wrong shall be perfectly and forever set right. He will finally assert Himself in overwhelming majesty and power com-

pelling all things to the issues of His own will. The final acts will
constitute the mighty and majestic march which will be in the
fullest sense the day of the Lord.

But oh, the sweet story of His grace! In His present dealings
with men the love of His heart is always a factor, but it never acts
at the expense of righteousness. Wherever the lesson of His
chastisement is learned and a man or a nation in penitence returns
to Him, His judgment is restrained in mercy. When you repent,
God repents. That is the great and gracious message of this
wonderful prophecy.

Then the *plan*. In any consideration of this message it is im-
portant to remember the place we occupy in the plan as declared.
We live in the day of the poured-out Spirit. It is a day of prophecy,
of dreams, of visions, and the things irrespective of caste or any human division. The ending of the day will be ushered in by signs and
portents mysterious and supernatural. During its course "whosoever shall call on the name of the Lord shall be saved." It is the
day of God's patience, preceding the putting forth of His power.

II. *Applied*. The application of this principle of government to
our day is so patent as to need few comments.

The principles. For life and service it is of the utmost importance that the heart should be warned and comforted by being constantly reminded of the present overruling of God, and
the sure certainty of His final victory. This is, as never before, the
day of *Man*. Progress, invention, culture, are helping to make man
imagine that he can do without God, and there is a tendency everywhere to deify human reason and human ability. The results are
disastrous to all that is highest and best in human possibility.
When these facts overwhelm us our hope is in the assurance that
the day of the Lord is now present and yet in all its majesty is yet
to come.

Our message to the age must always be that of the divine
supremacy, of the divine immanence, of the divine activity. We
want to tell men that the Lord that sitteth in the heavens laughs
at the folly of their rebellion, and weeps over the misery of their
sin, and waits as King to pardon repenting souls. Whenever men
and nations return to the Lord, His mercy receives them and
provides escape from judgment. That seems to me to be the great

and marvelous message of Joel to this age—the God of government and the God of grace.

The plan. It is for us to declare that the day of the Lord must come, but that we are living in the dispensation of the poured-out Spirit. We must urge men to call on the name of Jehovah, for only thus may they be saved from the perils, the judgments, of His coming day.

CHAPTER 3

AMOS *means Burden Bearer*

1 The words of Amos, who was among the herdmen of Tekoa, which he saw concerning Israel in the days of Uzziah king of Judah, and in the days of Jeroboam the son of Joash king of Israel, two years before the earthquake.

2 And he said, The Lord will roar from Zion, and utter his voice from Jerusalem; and the habitations of the shepherds shall mourn, and the top of Carmel shall wither.

3 Thus saith the Lord; For three transgressions of Damascus, and for four, I will not turn away the punishment thereof; because they have threshed Gilead with threshing instruments of iron:

4 But I will send a fire into the house of Hazael, which shall devour the palaces of Ben-hadad.

5 I will break also the bar of Damascus, and cut off the inhabitant from the plain of Aven, and him that holdeth the sceptre from the house of Eden: and the people of Syria shall go into captivity unto Kir, saith the Lord.

6 Thus saith the Lord; For three transgressions of Gaza, and for four, I will not turn away the punishment thereof; because they carried away captive the whole captivity, to deliver them up to Edom:

7 But I will send a fire on the wall of Gaza, which shall devour the palaces thereof:

8 And I will cut off the inhabitant from Ashdod, and him that holdeth the sceptre from Ashkelon, and I will turn mine hand against Ekron: and the remnant of the Philistines shall perish, saith the Lord God.

9 Thus saith the Lord; For three transgressions of Tyrus, and for four, I will not turn away the punishment thereof; because they delivered up the whole captivity to Edom, and remembered not the brotherly covenant:

10 But I will send a fire on the wall of Tyrus, which shall devour the palaces thereof.

11 Thus saith the Lord; For three transgressions of Edom, and for four, I will not turn away the punishment thereof; because he did pursue his brother with the sword, and did cast off all pity, and his anger did tear perpetually, and he kept his wrath for ever:

12 But I will send a fire upon Teman, which shall devour the palaces of Bozrah.

13 Thus saith the Lord; For three

transgressions of the children of Ammon, and for four, I will not turn away the punishment thereof; because they have ripped up the women with child, of Gilead, that they might enlarge their border:

14 But I will kindle a fire in the wall of Rabbah, and it shall devour the palaces thereof, with shouting in the day of battle, with a tempest in the day of the whirlwind:

15 And their king shall go into captivity, he and his princes together, saith the Lord.

CHAPTER 2

1 Thus saith the Lord; For three trangressions of Moab, and for four, I will not turn away the punishment thereof; because he burned the bones of the king of Edom into lime:

2 But I will send a fire upon Moab, and it shall devour the palaces of Kirioth: and Moab shall die with tumult, with shouting, and with the sound of the trumpet:

3 And I will cut off the judge from the midst thereof, and will slay all the princes thereof with him, saith the Lord.

4 Thus saith the Lord; For three transgressions of Judah, and for four, I will not turn away the punishment thereof; because they have despised the law of the Lord, and have not kept his commandments, and their lies caused them to err, after which their fathers have walked:

5 But I will send a fire upon Judah, and it shall devour the palaces of Jerusalem.

6 Thus saith the Lord; For three transgressions of Israel, and for four, I will not turn away the punishment thereof; because they sold the righteous for silver, and the poor for a pair of shoes;

7 That pant after the dust of the earth on the head of the poor, and turn aside the way of the meek: and a man and his father will go in unto the same maid, to profane my holy name:

8 And they lay themselves down upon clothes laid to pledge by every altar, and they drink the wine of the condemned in the house of their god.

9 Yet destroyed I the Amorite before them, whose height was like the height of the cedars, and he was strong as the oaks; yet I destroyed his fruit from above, and his roots from beneath.

10 Also I brought you up from the land of Egypt, and led you forty years through the wilderness, to possess the land of the Amorite.

11 And I raised up of your sons for prophets, and of your young men for Nazarites. Is it not even thus, O ye children of Israel? saith the Lord.

12 But ye gave the Nazarites wine to drink; and commanded the prophets, saying, Prophesy not.

13 Behold, I am pressed under you, as a cart is pressed that is full of sheaves.

14 Therefore the flight shall perish from the swift, and the strong shall not strengthen his force, neither shall the mighty deliver himself:

15 Neither shall he stand that handleth the bow; and he that is swift of foot shall not deliver himself: neither shall he that rideth the horse deliver himself.

16 And he that is courageous among the mighty shall flee away naked in that day, saith the Lord.

CHAPTER 3

1 Hear this word that the Lord hath spoken against you, O children of Israel, against the whole family which I brought up from the land of Egypt, saying,

2 You only have I known of all the families of the earth: therefore I will punish you for all your iniquities.

3 Can two walk together, except they be agreed?

4 Will a lion roar in the forest,

when he hath no prey? will a young lion cry out of his den, if he have taken nothing?

5 Can a bird fall in a snare upon the earth, where no gin is for him? shall one take up a snare from the earth, and have taken nothing at all?

6 Shall a trumpet be blown in the city, and the people not be afraid? shall there be evil in the city, and the Lord hath not done it?

7 Surely the Lord God will do nothing, but he revealeth his secret unto his servants the prophets.

8 The lion hath roared, who will not fear? the Lord God hath spoken, who can but prophesy?

9 Publish in the palaces at Ashdod, and in the palaces in the land of Egypt, and say, Assemble yourselves upon the mountains of Samaria, and behold the great tumults in the midst thereof, and the oppressed in the midst thereof.

10 For they know not to do right, saith the Lord, who store up violence and robbery in their palaces.

11 Therefore thus saith the Lord God; An adversary there shall be even round about the land; and he shall bring down thy strength from thee, and thy palaces shall be spoiled.

12 Thus saith the Lord; As the shepherd taketh out of the mouth of the lion two legs, or a piece of an ear; so shall the children of Israel be taken out that dwell in Samaria in the corner of a bed, and in Damascus in a couch.

13 Hear ye, and testify in the house of Jacob, saith the Lord God, the God of hosts.

14 That, in the day that I shall visit the transgressions of Israel upon him, I will also visit the altars of Bethel: and the horns of the altar shall be cut off, and fall to the ground.

15 And I will smite the winter house with the summer house; and the houses of ivory shall perish, and the great houses shall have an end, saith the Lord.

CHAPTER 4

1 Hear this word, ye kine of Bashan, that are in the mountain of Samaria, which oppress the poor, which crush the needy, which say to their masters, Bring and let us drink.

2 The Lord God hath sworn by his holiness, that, lo, the days shall come upon you, that he will take you away with hooks, and your posterity with fishhooks.

3 And ye shall go out at the breaches, every cow at that which is before her; and ye shall cast them into the palace, saith the Lord.

4 Come to Bethel, and transgress; at Gilgal multiply transgression; and bring your sacrifices every morning, and your tithes after three years:

5 And offer a sacrifice of thanksgiving with leaven, and proclaim and publish the free offerings: for this liketh you, O ye children of Israel, saith the Lord God.

6 And I also have given you cleanness of teeth in all your cities, and want of bread in all your places: yet have ye not returned unto me, saith the Lord.

7 And also I have withholden the rain from you, when there were yet three months to the harvest: and I caused it to rain upon one city, and caused it not to rain upon another city: one piece was rained upon, and the piece whereupon it rained not withered.

8 So two or three cities wandered unto one city, to drink water; but they were not satisfied: yet have ye not returned unto me saith the Lord.

9 I have smitten you with blasting and mildew: when your gardens and your vineyards and your fig trees and your olive trees increased, the palmerworm devoured them: yet have ye not returned unto me, saith the Lord.

10 I have sent among you the pestilence after the manner of Egypt: your young men have I slain with the sword, and have taken away your horses; and I have made the stink

of your camps to come up unto your nostrils: yet have ye not returned unto me, saith the Lord.

11 I have overthrown some of you, as God overthrew Sodom and Gomorrah, and ye were as a firebrand plucked out of the burning: yet have ye not returned unto me, saith the Lord.

12 Therefore thus will I do unto thee, O Israel: and because I will do this unto thee, prepare to meet thy God, O Israel.

13 For, lo, he that formeth the mountains, and createth the wind, and declareth unto man what is his thought, that maketh the morning darkness, and treadeth upon the high places of the earth, The Lord, The God of hosts, is his name.

CHAPTER 5

1 Hear ye this word which I take up against you, even a lamentation, O house of Israel.

2 The virgin of Israel is fallen; she shall no more rise: she is forsaken upon her land; there is none to raise her up.

3 For thus saith the Lord God; The city that went out by a thousand shall leave a hundred, and that which went forth by a hundred shall leave ten, to the house of Israel.

4 For thus saith the Lord unto the house of Israel, Seek ye me, and ye shall live:

5 But seek not Bethel, nor enter into Gilgal, and pass not to Beersheba: for Gilgal shall surely go into captivity, and Bethel shall come to nought.

6 Seek the Lord, and ye shall live; lest he break out like fire in the house of Joseph, and devour it, and there be none to quench it in Bethel.

7 Ye who turn judgment to wormwood, and leave off righteousness in the earth,

8 Seek him that maketh the seven stars and Orion, and turneth the shadow of death into the morning,

and maketh the day dark with night: that calleth for the waters of the sea, and poureth them out upon the face of the earth: The Lord is his name.

9 That strengtheneth the spoiled against the strong, so that the spoiled shall come against the fortress.

10 They hate him that rebuketh in the gate, and they abhor him that speaketh uprightly.

11 Forasmuch therefore as your treading is upon the poor, and ye take from him burdens of wheat: ye have built houses of hewn stone, but ye shall not dwell in them; ye have planted pleasant vineyards, but ye shall not drink wine from them.

12 For I know your manifold transgressions and your mighty sins: they afflict the just, they take a bribe, and they turn aside the poor in the gate from their right.

13 Therefore the prudent shall keep silence in that time; for it is an evil time.

14 Seek good, and not evil, that ye may live: and so the Lord, the God of hosts, shall be with you, as ye have spoken.

15 Hate the evil, and love the good, and establish judgment in the gate: it may be that the Lord God of hosts will be gracious unto the remnant of Joseph.

16 Therefore the Lord, the God of hosts, the Lord, saith thus; Wailing shall be in all streets; and they shall say in all the highways, Alas! alas! and they shall call the husbandman to mourning, and such as are skilful of lamentation to wailing.

17 And in all vineyards shall be wailing: for I will pass through thee, saith the Lord.

18 Woe unto you that desire the day of the Lord! to what end is it for you? the day of the Lord is darkness, and not light.

19 As if a man did flee from a lion, and a bear met him; or went into the house, and leaned his hand on the wall, and a serpent bit him.

20 Shall not the day of the Lord be darkness, and not light? even very dark, and no brightness in it?

21 I hate, I despise your feast days, and I will not smell in your solemn assemblies.

22 Though ye offer me burnt offerings and your meat offerings, I will not accept them; neither will I regard the peace offerings of your fat beasts.

23 Take thou away from me the noise of thy songs; for I will not hear the melody of thy viols.

24 But let judgment run down as waters, and righteousness as a mighty stream.

25 Have ye offered unto me sacrifices and offerings in the wilderness forty years, O house of Israel?

26 But ye have borne the tabernacle of your Moloch and Chiun your images, the star of your god, which ye made to yourselves.

27 Therefore will I cause you to go into captivity beyond Damascus, saith the Lord, whose name is The God of hosts.

CHAPTER 6

1 Woe to them that are at ease in Zion, and trust in the mountain of Samaria, which are named chief of the nations, to whom the house of Israel came!

2 Pass ye unto Calneh, and see; and from thence go ye to Hamath the great: then go down to Gath of the Philistines: be they better than these kingdoms? or their border greater than your border?

3 Ye that put far away the evil day, and cause the seat of violence to come near;

4 That lie upon beds of ivory, and stretch themselves upon their couches, and eat the lambs out of the flock, and the calves out of the midst of the stall;

5 That chant to the sound of the viol, and invent to themselves instruments of music, like David;

6 That drink wine in bowls, and anoint themselves with the chief ointments: but they are not grieved for the affliction of Joseph.

7 Therefore now shall they go captive with the first that go captive, and the banquet of them that stretched themselves shall be removed.

8 The Lord God hath sworn by himself, saith the Lord the God of hosts, I abhor the excellency of Jacob, and hate his palaces: therefore will I deliver up the city with all that is therein.

9 And it shall come to pass, if there remain ten men in one house, that they shall die.

10 And a man's uncle shall take him up, and he that burneth him, to bring out the bones out of the house, and shall say unto him that is by the sides of the house, Is there yet any with thee? and he shall say, No. Then shall he say, Hold thy tongue: for we may not make mention of the name of the Lord.

11 For, behold, the Lord commandeth, and he will smite the great house with breaches, and the little house with clefts.

12 Shall horses run upon the rock? will one plow there with oxen? for ye have turned judgment into gall, and the fruit of righteousness into hemlock:

13 Ye which rejoice in a thing of nought, which say, Have we not taken to us horns by our own strength?

14 But, behold, I will raise up against you a nation, O house of Israel, saith the Lord the God of hosts; and they shall afflict you from the entering in of Hamath unto the river of the wilderness.

CHAPTER 7

1 Thus hath the Lord God showed unto me; and, behold, he formed grasshoppers in the beginning of the

shooting up of the latter growth; and, lo, it was the latter growth after the king's mowings.

2 And it came to pass, that when they had made an end of eating the grass of the land, then I said, O Lord God, forgive, I beseech thee: by whom shall Jacob arise? for he is small.

3 The Lord repented for this: It shall not be, saith the Lord.

4 Thus hath the Lord God showed unto me: and, behold, the Lord God called to contend by fire, and it devoured the great deep, and did eat up a part.

5 Then said I, O Lord God, cease, I beseech thee: by whom shall Jacob arise? for he is small.

6 The Lord repented for this: This also shall not be, saith the Lord God.

7 Thus he showed me: and, behold, the Lord stood upon a wall made by a plumbline, with a plumbline in his hand.

8 And the Lord said unto me, Amos, what seest thou? And I said, A plumbline. Then said the Lord, Behold, I will set a plumbline in the midst of my people Israel: I will not again pass by them any more:

9 And the high places of Isaac shall be desolate, and the sanctuaries of Israel shall be laid waste; and I will rise against the house of Jeroboam with the sword.

10 Then Amaziah the priest of Bethel sent to Jeroboam king of Israel, saying, Amos hath conspired against thee in the midst of the house of Israel: the land is not able to bear all his words.

11 For thus Amos saith, Jeroboam shall die by the sword, and Israel shall surely be led away captive out of their own land.

12 Also Amaziah said unto Amos, O thou seer, go, flee thee away into the land of Judah, and there eat bread, and prophesy there:

13 But prophesy not again any more at Bethel: for it is the king's chapel, and it is the king's court.

14 Then answered Amos, and said to Amaziah, I was no prophet, neither was I a prophet's son; but I was a herdman, and a gatherer of sycamore fruit:

15 And the Lord took me as I followed the flock, and the Lord said unto me, Go, prophesy unto my people Israel.

16 Now therefore hear thou the word of the Lord: Thou sayest, Prophesy not against Israel, and drop not thy word against the house of Isaac.

17 Therefore thus saith the Lord; Thy wife shall be a harlot in the city, and thy sons and thy daughters shall fall by the sword, and thy land shall be divided by line; and thou shalt die in a polluted land: and Israel shall surely go into captivity forth of his land.

CHAPTER 8

1 Thus hath the Lord God showed unto me: and behold a basket of summer fruit.

2 And he said, Amos, what seest thou? And I said, A basket of summer fruit. Then said the Lord unto me, The end is come upon my people of Israel; I will not again pass by them any more.

3 And the songs of the temple shall be howlings in that day, saith the Lord God: there shall be many dead bodies in every place; they shall cast them forth with silence.

4 Hear this, O ye that swallow up the needy, even to make the poor of the land to fail,

5 Saying, When will the new moon be gone, that we may sell corn? and the sabbath, that we may set forth wheat, making the ephah small, and the shekel great, and falsifying the balances by deceit?

6 That we may buy the poor for silver, and the needy for a pair of

shoes; yea, and sell the refuse of the wheat?

7 The Lord hath sworn by the excellency of Jacob, Surely I will never forget any of their works.

8 Shall not the land tremble for this, and every one mourn that dwelleth therein? and it shall rise up wholly as a flood; and it shall be cast out and drowned, as by the flood of Egypt.

9 And it shall come to pass in that day, saith the Lord God, that I will cause the sun to go down at noon, and I will darken the earth in the clear day:

10 And I will turn your feasts into mourning, and all your songs into lamentation; and I will bring up sackcloth upon all loins, and baldness upon every head; and I will make it as the mourning of an only son, and the end thereof as a bitter day.

11 Behold, the days come, saith the Lord God, that I will send a famine in the land, not a famine of bread, nor a thirst for water, but of hearing the words of the Lord:

12 And they shall wander from sea to sea, and from the north even to the east, they shall run to and fro to seek the word of the Lord, and shall not find it.

13 In that day shall the fair virgins and young men faint for thirst.

14 They that swear by the sin of Samaria, and say, Thy god, O Dan, liveth; and, The manner of Beer-she-ba liveth; even they shall fall, and never rise up again.

CHAPTER 9

1 I saw the Lord standing upon the altar: and he said, Smite the lintel of the door, that the posts may shake: and cut them in the head, all of them; and I will slay the last of them with the sword: he that fleeth of them shall not flee away, and he that escapeth of them shall not be delivered.

2 Though they dig into hell, thence shall mine hand take them; though they climb up to heaven, thence will I bring them down:

3 And though they hide themselves in the top of Carmel, I will search and take them out thence; and though they be hid from my sight in the bottom of the sea, thence will I command the serpent, and he shall bite them:

4 And though they go into captivity before their enemies, thence will I command the sword, and it shall slay them: and I will set mine eyes upon them for evil, and not for good.

5 And the Lord God of hosts is he that toucheth the land, and it shall melt, and all that dwell therein shall mourn: and it shall rise up wholly like a flood; and shall be drowned, as by the flood of Egypt.

6 It is he that buildeth his stories in the heaven, and hath founded his troop in the earth; he that calleth for the waters of the sea, and poureth them out upon the face of the earth: The Lord is his name.

7 Are ye not as children of the Ethiopians unto me, O children of Israel? saith the Lord. Have not I brought up Israel out of the land of Egypt? and the Philistines from Caphtor, and the Syrians from Kir?

8 Behold, the eyes of the Lord God are upon the sinful kingdom, and I will destroy it from off the face of the earth; saving that I will not utterly destroy the house of Jacob, saith the Lord.

9 For, lo, I will command, and I will sift the house of Israel among all nations, like as corn is sifted in a sieve, yet shall not the least grain fall upon the earth.

10 All sinners of my people shall die by the sword, which say, The evil shall not overtake nor prevent us.

11 In that day will I raise up the tabernacle of David that is fallen, and close up the breaches thereof; and I

will raise up his ruins, and I will build it as in the days of old:

12 That they may possess the remnant of Edom, and of all the heathen, which are called by my name, saith the Lord that doeth this.

13 Behold, the days come, saith the Lord, that the plowman shall overtake the reaper, and the treader of grapes him that soweth seed; and the mountains shall drop sweet wine, and all the hills shall melt.

14 And I will bring again the captivity of my people of Israel, and they shall build the waste cities, and inhabit them; and they shall plant vineyards, and drink the wine thereof; they shall also make gardens, and eat the fruit of them.

15 And I will plant them upon their land, and they shall no more be pulled up out of their land which I have given them, saith the Lord thy God.

AMOS—NATIONAL ACCOUNTABILITY

A. The Prophet and His Times

I. *Dates.* Amos was partly contemporaneous with Hosea. In the reign of Jeroboam he came out of Tekoah, in Judah, to Bethel, in Israel. The exact date cannot be fixed, but his message was delivered two years before the earthquake (Amos 1:1), as he declares when committing those messages to writing. This earthquake is noticed by Zechariah (14:5), and Josephus places it at the time when Uzziah was smitten with leprosy (II Chronicles 26:16–21). In all probability the messages of Amos were delivered during the period when Jeroboam was king of Israel and Uzziah king of Judah; when Hosea was beginning his long career of prophesying.

II. *Characteristics.* The later years of the reign of Jeroboam were characterized by great material prosperity. There are evidences in his message of the wealth and luxury of the people. (See 3:15, 5:11, 6:4–8.) These same references show, as do many others, that injustice, oppression and vice were rampant, the poor being ground down under the heel of the rich. These very material tokens of prosperity were being construed by the people into signs of the special evidences of divine protection, and yet they were forgetful of the requirements of His law.

B. The Analysis of the Prophecy

I. *Declamations* (*chapters 1, 2*).

The second verse of this first chapter gives us the key to the book. By it we are introduced to the true standpoint: Jehovah declaring Himself in judgment. This first section consists of the declarations concerning the doom of the derelicts. All nations are seen passing before Jehovah and receiving sentence. The key is "Thus saith the Lord."

a. Damascus, Syria (1:3–5).
    1. The announcement:
        (a) Divine. "Thus saith the Lord."
        (b) Fullness of sin: "Three—yea, four!"
        (c) Punishment must now come.
    2. The reason: Cruelty.
    3. The sentence: The flame to devour; defense to be useless (the bar broken); the rout of the people into captivity.
b. Gaza, Philistia (1:6–8).
    1. The announcement (this is repeated each time as before).
    2. The reason: The slave trade.
    3. The sentence: the flame to devour; the inhabitants to be cut off; the remnant to perish.
c. Tyre, Phoenicia (1:9, 10).
    1. The announcement.
    2. The reason: Slave agents in spite of a covenant.
    3. The sentence: The flame to devour.
d. Edom (1:11, 12).
    1. The announcement.
    2. The reason: Determined and revengeful unforgiveness.
    3. The sentence: The flame to devour.
e. Children of Ammon (1:13–15).
    1. The announcement.
    2. The reason: Cruelty based on cupidity.
    3. The sentence: The flame to devour; with shouting and tempest; the king and princes carried into captivity.
f. Moab (2:1–3).
    1. The announcement.
    2. The reason: Shocking and vindictive hatred.

3. The sentence: The flame to devour; die with shouting, tumult, trumpet; cut off the judge and slay the princes.

g. Judah (2:4, 5).
1. The announcement.
2. The reason: Despised the law of Jehovah; kept not His statutes; lies caused them to err.
3. The sentence: The flame to devour.

h. Israel (2:6–16).
1. The announcement.
2. The reason:
(a) The charges: (1) Injustice; (2) avarice; (3) oppression; (4) immorality; (5) profanity; (6) blasphemy; (7) sacrilege.
(b) Aggravation of the sin: (1) The Amorites destroyed before them; (2) brought up out of Egypt; (3) raised up sons for prophets and young men for Nazarites; (4) these corrupted.
3. The sentence:
(a) Pressure of judgment. (b) Impossibility of escape.

II. Proclamations (chapters 3—4).

Having thus issued the declamations of Jehovah's judgment upon all the nations, the prophet now proceeds to deliver his special message to Israel. This is done in a series of three discourses. In each the introductory word is, "Hear this Word" (3:1; 4:1; 5:1).

a. Discourse I. Jehovah's verdict and sentence (chapter 3).
1. The privileged people to be punished (3:1, 2). This is first simply stated:
(a) Those addressed.
(b) Their privileges.
(c) Their punishment.
2. The prophet's vindication of himself (3:3–8). This is an interpolation in which the prophet defends himself against the probable objections of the people.
(a) Declaration of principle. An effect proves a cause. This is argued in a series of seven questions.
(b) Deduction from the principle. (1) Jehovah hath

roared, therefore fear. (2) Jehovah hath spoken, therefore the prophecy.
3. The punishment of the privileged, and its reason (3:9–15).
   (a) The reason declared to the heathen who are invited to witness the justice of the doom.
   (b) The doom.
b. Discourse II. Jehovah's summons (chapter 4).
   1. The indictment of the women (4:1–3).
      (a) "Ye kine of Basham." The degradation of womanhood to mere animalism. An awful revelation.
      (b) Their doings: Oppress the poor; crush the needy; drink.
      (c) Their doom: "Taken away with hooks"; "Go out at the breaches.
   2. The final summons to the people (4:4–13).
      (a) The satire (verses 4, 5). To Bethel—to transgress. To Gilgal—to multiply transgression. Sacrifices— every morning instead of once a year. Tithe—every third day instead of third year. Sacrifice—leavened. Free-will offerings—publish them! "This liketh you!"
      (b) God's patience and their perversity (verses 6–11). "Yet have ye not returned unto me."
      (c) The summons (4:12, 13).
c. Discourse III. Lamentation and its causes (chapters 5, 6).
   1. The lamentation over the virgin of Israel (verses 1, 2).
   2. The sequence of explanations. Introduced with "Thus saith the Lord" (verses 3–17).
      (a) "Thus saith the Lord." The fact declared of the diminution of the number of the people (verse 3).
      (b) "Thus saith the Lord" (verses 4–15). Again the history of God's past calls. (1) The call. (2) The refusal. (3) The results. (4) Yet another call.
      (c) "Thus saith the Lord" (verses 16, 17). The consequent doom. "I will pass through the midst of thee."
   3. The double woe (5:18—6).
      (a) "Those who desire the day of the Lord" (verses 18–27). The hypocrites. God says: "I hate . . . I despise . . . I take no delight . . . I will not accept . . . I will not regard . . . I will not hear." His call

is for righteousness and judgment. His day for them
will be destruction and darkness.

(b) "Those at ease in Zion" (chapter 6). The indifferent.

III. Revelations (chapters 7—9).

A fourfold vision of judgment introduced in each case with the
words "The Lord shewed me," except in the last, where the vision
is of the Lord Himself.

a. Vision I (7:1–3). The Locusts. Judgment threatened and re-
    strained.
    1. The symbol: Locusts eating up the grass.
    2. The intercession: "O Lord God, forgive I beseech thee."
    3. The answer: Jehovah repented. This word indicates the
        sorrow of God. He arrested the judgment.
b. Vision II (7:4–6). The Fire. Judgment threatened and re-
    strained.
    1. The symbol: The devouring fire.
    2. The intercession: "O Lord God, cease I beseech thee."
    3. The answer: The same repentance. "This also shall not be."
c. Vision III (7:7–9). The Plumbline. Judgment determined.
    1. The symbol: The plumbline of rectitude; the appeal to
        Amos; no charge is made, but it is evident that as Amos
        beheld, he realized all the irregularities the plumbline
        revealed.
    2. Doom determined. No more restraint.
d. Historical interpolation (7:10–17). So long as the prophecy
    was mingled with a message of mercy, it was tolerated. Now
    that element is missing, hostility breaks out.
    1. Amaziah.
        (a) An imposture as priest of Bethel.
        (b) Message to Jeroboam, reporting to him and advising
            the exile of Amos.
        (c) Message to Amos, advising him to flee to Judah by
            appealing to his fear.
    2. Amos.
        (a) Declares his authority.
        (b) Answers Amaziah, threatening with personal and
            national disaster.

e. Vision IV (chapter 8). Basket of Summer Fruit. Judgment at
   hand.
   1. The symbol (verse 1). "A basket of Kaitz. . . . Ketz has
      come." The Hebrew words for summer fruit and for end
      are almost identical. The basket of fruit is evidently the
      symbol of Israel's ripeness for judgment.
   2. The announcement (verses 2, 3). "The end is come."
   3. The prophet's application (verses 4–14).
      (a) Impassioned address to the money makers (verses
          4–6). The effect, the intensity and the method of
          their lust for gain.
      (b) Figurative description of the judgment (verses 9, 10).
          (1) Jehovah's consciousness. (2) Jehovah's retribu-
          tion.
      (c) The final issue of judgment (verses 11–14). (1) Fam-
          ine of the words of the Lord. (2) Eager and fruitless
          search. (3) Fainting of youth for lack. (4) The
          reason of all: Acceptance of the false has issued in
          lack of the true.
f. Vision V (9:1–10). Jehovah. Judgment executed. Here there
   is no symbol, no sign, but the present acting, smiting Jehovah.
   It is one of the most awe-inspiring visions of the whole Bible.
   The message proceeds in two phases:
   1. Judgment irrevocable and irresistible (9:1–6).
      (a) The vision. Jehovah standing by the altar.
      (b) The words: The stroke of destruction; the futile at-
          tempts at escape; the divine self-assertion.
   2. Judgment reasonable and discriminative (9:7–10).
      (a) The claims in which Israel had trusted are nothing:
          They had become as children of Ethiopians; Philis-
          tines and Syrians had also been led by God.
      (b) Jehovah's eyes are on the sinful kingdom: For sin
          they are punished like heathen.
      (c) Saving utter destruction: The sifting must be; no
          grain shall perish.

IV. Restoration (9:11–15).

The opening phrase "in that day" connects this closing message
of restoration with all that has preceded it. Here it is declared

that the reason of the divine judgment is not revenge, but that
it is the only way in which it is possible to usher in the divine order
upon which the head of God is ever set. The key to the passage is
in the sequence between the "I will" and the "They shall."

a. Restoration. Initial (9:11-13).
    1. "I will."
        (a) "Raise up the tabernacle of David that is fallen."
        (b) "And close up the breaches thereof."
        (c) "Raise up his ruins."
        (d) "Build it as in the days of old."
    2. "That they may."
        (a) Possession according to purpose. Note this return
            to divine purpose.
        (b) Prosperity.
b. Restoration. Progressive (verse 14).
    1. "I will . . . bring again the captivity of my people Israel."
    2. "They shall."
        (a) "Build the waste cities and inhabit them." The human
            working of the divine victory.
        (b) "Plant vineyards . . . and drink wine." Human toil
            realizing divine provision.
        (c) "Make gardens . . . and eat the fruit." Human ap-
            propriation of divine preparation.

Note. The contrast is between the divine government and captivity. Now they possess and enjoy the results of their toil.

c. Restoration. Permanent (verse 15).
    1. "I will." "Plant them." The declaration of God's determina-
        tion to carry out His original design.
    2. "They shall." "No more be plucked up." The declaration of
        the security of those established by God, against all foes.

THE MESSAGE OF AMOS

So far as his message to the time was concerned, Amos first of all
revealed to Israel the startling truth that God was interested in all
the nations round about as well as in Israel. They, too, were
responsible to Him and under His control. The prophet began
with Damascus and with all those surrounding nations, and de-

clared that Judah and Israel had sinned and therefore they were
judged on the same basis as the other nations.

Then came the startling anouncement that the judgment of
Judah and Israel was to be more severe than those outside nations,
because the light of Judah and Israel had been far more clear in
its shining. Special privileges create special responsibilities and
the neglect of them brings greater condemnation.

The message of Amos is cumulative, like the sweep of an ava-
lanche, and its most emphatic note is that the divine judgment can
only be averted by a return to the pathway of obedience. From
general declamations to personal proclamations, he passes the
searching revelations of coming judgment until at last Jehovah is
seen in all the terror of outraged patience smiting the rebellious
people.

Yet the last word swells with the music of the victory of love.
None are destroyed but the sinners and, through the awful process
of judgment rendered necessary by long continued rebellion, God
restores and finally realizes all the purposes of His love.

C. The Permanent Message

I. *Stated.* If the prophecy teaches us anything it is this: Jehovah
still governs among the nations and will deal with them as nations.
No national sin goes unobserved or unpunished. It is true that He
has formed a holy nation and is dealing with the holy nation, but
it is an utterly mistaken idea to imagine that meanwhile He has
forgotten the other nations. He has never handed over the reins
of government. Today the righteousness of a nation insures the
blessings of Jehovah, and the sin of a nation insures the judgment
and curse of Jehovah.

Then, as a sequence, we may say that those nations that have
clearest light have greatest responsibility. As sins against clear
light are more heinous than those committed in twilight, so will
the judgment of those that sin against clear light be more terrible
"Why," said Jesus to Capernaum and Chorazin, "if Sodom anc
Gommorrah had seen the light you have seen, they would have
repented and would have been saved." If that be true, I suggest to
you a statement that brings that principle down to this hour: it
shall be more tolerable for Capernaum, for Chorazin, for Jeru-

salem, than for New York, and Philadelphia, and Chicago. But, you say, those cities had Christ in person. I tell you the light was not half as bright there as it is in our cities today. He was then the localized, the limited, the misunderstood Christ, but today He is unlocalized, unlimited, and the Spirit of Christ has appealed to the nations; and we know, in spite of all our base denials, that His voice is authoritative, that His law is the highest. If we disregard it, our judgment will be more terrible than the judgment of Chorazin, and Capernaum, and Jerusalem. This is a national truth that we must keep in mind.

No new philosophy will excuse nations that trifle with divine requirements; the walls of doom close slowly, surely, around all those who forget God. These movements of terror are necessary to, and will issue in, the victory of God. Let the watchers and the waiters take heart; out of all the ruin and the wreckage, He will bring again His divine order.

II. *Applied.* In making application of this message let me remind you of the catalogue of national sins hateful to God among nations which we find in Amos.

The sin of Syria—cruelty.

The sin of Philistia—the slave trade.

The sin of Phoenicia—slave agents in spite of covenant.

The sin of Edom—determined unforgiveness.

The sin of Ammon—cruelty based upon cupidity.

The sin of Moab—violent and vindictive hatred.

The sin of Judah—Jehovah's laws despised.

The sin of Israel—the corruption of a delivered people.

These are the national sins that God has set His face against, and oh, men and women, my brothers and sisters of the holy nation, let us never forget that Jehovah still holds the balance of even justice, and He is still against these things.

Now hear me. The people chosen to be the depository of truth have most tremendous responsibility. When we make our boast of the divine calling of the Anglo-Saxon people by creation and preservation, let us also bewail our sins, and let us cry aloud, and spare not against our corrupting of the covenant. I am one of those who believe most strongly that God has in these days created the Anglo-Saxon race, strangest of all strange mixtures as to its making, most marvelous and mighty of all people in the fact of its having been made, and God has made us the depository of truth, has committed to us a missionary responsibility. But oh, what a fall there will be unless we are true to these ideals as a race; and every man who loves his nation and loves the great race of which he forms a part owes it to the race and to his God that he never spares to cry aloud against the sins of materialism and all the things that threaten to corrupt the covenant that God has committed to us.

There can be no escape from doom but by the way of penitence. We are not yet independent of God, our inventions and our policies and our armaments and our combines notwithstanding.

That is the message that we have to preach, and the message that we have to live in the midst of the nation. Nevertheless let all the hearts of the loyal be established. Not for utter destruction does He destroy, but for the restoration and the victory of love among the sons of men.

To the "Holy Nation," of course, these messages have their special significance. She above all must give no countenance to the national sins which are hateful to Jehovah, for her light is most perfect. Let her above all others rejoice in the final victory of which she is most perfectly assured, having in Jesus had "the word of prophecy made more sure." Let her message be clear and unmistakable to the day in which she lives, and let it be a message of the throne of God and the relation of men to that throne in submission for permanence and for blessing.

CHAPTER 4

OBADIAH

1 The vision of Obadiah. Thus saith the Lord God concerning Edom; We have heard a rumor from the Lord, and an ambassador is sent among the heathen, Arise ye, and let us rise up against her in battle.

2 Behold, I have made thee small among the heathen: thou art greatly despised.

3 The pride of thine heart hath deceived thee, thou that dwellest in the clefts of the rock, whose habitation is high; that saith in his heart, Who shall bring me down to the ground?

4 Though thou exalt thyself as the eagle, and though thou set thy nest among the stars, thence will I bring thee down, saith the Lord.

5 If thieves came to thee, if robbers by night, (how art thou cut off!) would they not have stolen till they had enough? if the grape gatherers came to thee, would they not leave some grapes?

6 How are the things of Esau searched out! how are his hidden things sought up!

7 All the men of thy confederacy have brought thee even to the border: the men that were at peace with thee have deceivd thee, and prevailed against thee; they that eat thy bread have laid a wound under thee: there is none understanding in him.

8 Shall I not in that day, saith the Lord, even destroy the wise men out of Edom, and understanding out of the mount of Esau?

9 And thy mighty men, O Teman, shall be dismayed, to the end that every one of the mount of Esau may be cut off by slaughter.

10 For thy violence against thy brother Jacob shame shall cover thee, and thou shalt be cut off for ever.

11 In the day that thou stoodest on the other side, in the day that the strangers carried away captive his forces, and foreigners entered into his gates, and cast lots upon Jerusalem, even thou wast as one of them.

12 But thou shouldest not have looked on the day of thy brother in the day that he became a stranger; neither shouldest thou have rejoiced over the children of Judah in the day of their destruction; neither shouldest thou have spoken proudly in the day of distress.

13 Thou shouldest not have entered into the gate of my people in the day of their calamity; yea, thou shouldest not have looked on their affliction in the day of their calamity, nor have laid hands on their substance in the day of their calamity.

14 Neither shouldest thou have stood in the crossway, to cut off those of his that did escape; neither shouldest thou have delivered up those of his that did remain in the day of distress.

15 For the day of the Lord is near upon all the heathen: as thou hast done, it shall be done unto thee: thy reward shall return upon thine own head.

16 For as ye have drunk upon my holy mountain, so shall all the heathen drink continually; yea, they shall drink, and they shall swallow down, and they shall be as though they had not been.

17 But upon mount Zion shall be deliverance, and there shall be holiness; and the house of Jacob shall possess their possessions.

18 And the house of Jacob shall be a fire, and the house of Joseph a flame, and the house of Esau for stubble, and they shall kindle in them, and devour them; and there shall not be any remaining of the house of Esau; for the Lord hath spoken it.

19 And they of the south shall possess the mount of Esau; and they of the plain, the Philistines: and they shall possess the fields of Ephraim, and the fields of Samaria: and Benjamin shall possess Gilead.

20 And the captivity of this host of the children of Israel shall possess that of the Canaanites, even unto Zarephath; and the captivity of Jerusalem, which is in Sepharad, shall possess the cities of the south.

21 And saviours shall come up on mount Zion to judge the mount of Esau; and the kingdom shall be the Lord's.

OBADIAH—THE CURSE OF COWARDICE

A. The Prophet and His Times

I. *Dates.* There is no personal history of Obadiah, and it is therefore impossible to fix the date accurately. The only ground is that of the capture of Jerusalem to which reference is so clearly made. Certain passages in Jeremiah apparently quoted from this book make it seem that Obadiah refers to the capture of the city by Nebuchadnezzar. (Compare Obadiah 1:5 with Jeremiah 49:7–22.) The corrected tense of verses 12–14 in the Revised Version, "Look not" instead of "Thou shouldest not have looked," etc., would indicate that the prophecy was uttered before the fall of Jerusalem and not after it.

Obadiah quotes from Joel (compare verse 15 with 1:15; verse 17 with 3:17 and 2:32), also from Amos (compare verse 19 with 9:12), and from no later prophet. These facts place the prophecy approximately.

II. *Characteristics.* The nation was a hive of political disturbances, the people were divided into factions and parties. Fierce passions characterized these parties and evil counsels prevailed. The whole nation was rushing headlong toward a great catastrophe. Obadiah is given a vision of the attitude of Edom toward the chosen people in their calamity, and his message is delivered concerning Edom.

B. THE ANALYSIS OF THE PROPHECY

I. *Explanatory introduction (verse 1).*

a.   The method of communication: "The vision of Obadiah."
b.   The value of the message: "Thus saith the Lord God."
c.   The subject of the message: "Concerning Edom."
d.   A confirmatory coincidence: (1) "Tidings from the Lord."
      (2) "An ambassador," etc.

This is a peculiarly dignified and authoritative introduction. The tidings from the Lord are now to be declared. The events of the time ratify the message. There is a movement among the nations, against the chosen people.

II. *The judgment of Edom (verses 2–16).*

a.   The doom declared (verses 2–9).
    1.   First address of Jehovah (verses 2–4).
       (a)   Asserts His act.
       (b)   Declares the proud attitude of Edom.
       (c)   Announces His superior power.
    2.   Commentary of the prophet (verses 5–7).
       (a)   Exclamations: (1) "If!" An argument as to the utter ruin pending. (2) "How!" Even the prophet is astonished.
       (b)   Address to Edom. The events and men on which Edom trusted are working Jehovah's will.
       (c)   Contemplative exclamation. "There is none understanding in him!"
    3.   Second address of Jehovah (verses 8, 9).
       (a)   Destruction of the wise men.
       (b)   Dismay of the mighty.

b. The reason assigned (verses 10–16).
  1. The facts stated (verses 10–11).
    (a) Violence done to Jacob.
    (b) In Jacob's trouble, (1) Edom stood aloof and (2) joined the enemies.
  2. Descriptive analysis (verses 12–14).
    Day of disaster—look.
    Day of destruction—rejoice.
    Day of distress—speak proudly.
    Day of calamity—enter gate.
    Day of calamity—look on affliction.
    Day of calamity—lay hands on substance.
    Day of distress—cut off escape and deliver up.
  3. Retribution (verses 15, 16). "The day of the Lord. . . ."
    "As thou hast done, it shall be done unto thee."

III. The restoration of Israel (verses 17–21).

a. The delivered remnant (verse 17).
  1. Those that escape in Mount Zion.
  2. Mount Zion holy.
  3. House of Jacob possessing its own.
b. The victorious people (verse 18).
  1. Jacob a fire.
  2. Joseph a flame.
  3. Esau stubble.
c. The conquering people.
  1. Of the south.
  2. Of the lowland.
  3. "They. . . ."
  4. Benjamin (compare here Joshua 15).
d. The returning captives.
  1. Among the Canaanites.
  2. In Sepharad.
e. The final issue.
  1. Saviour on Mount Zion.
  2. To Judge Esau.
  3. "The kingdom shall be the Lord's." That is ever the final word!

The Message of Obadiah

The prophecy concerning Edom was spoken not to Edom, but to Israel, and would be intended especially as a word of comfort for those among the chosen people who, loyal to Jehovah, were yet suffering with the whole nation. It was a declaration of the fact that God is never unmindful of the actions of the enemies who take advantage of Israel's calamity, and the punishment of such was sure.

C. The Permanent Message

Is there any message of permanent value in this short half-page prophecy? I venture to think that there is. There may be very many lessons, but I take one only: God has never utterly cast off His ancient people Israel. Those nations which add personal insult and injury to them in the days of their chastisement will be held accountable by Him. The doom of the nation is sealed if, in its national capacity, it oppresses the ancient people.

These principles are, of course, of far more wide reaching application. The spirit of greed and cruelty is forever hateful to Jehovah, and so surely as any nation is actuated thereby in her dealings with other nations, by the Nemesis of God's judgments so shall she perish sooner or later.

Let the great powers of today remember that the measure of a nation's patience with God's suffering Israel is the measure of that nation's permanence. God is utterly unchangeable. You may boast of the armaments of the persecuting people; you may tell me of her gathered millions ready for battle. I care nothing. If she lift her hand against God's chosen people Israel, the very element of destruction is already at work within her; and though she build her nest among the stars, God will bring her down. The "Holy Nation," of which we form a part by God's grace, is peculiarly called to express the pitifulness of His heart even toward those who are suffering the calamities of His judgment.

One clear light ever burns ahead, leading us upward and onward; it is perfectly expressed in the closing words of Obadiah. "The kingdom shall be the Lord's."

CHAPTER 5

JONAH

CHAPTER 1

1 Now the word of the Lord came unto Jonah the son of Amittai, saying,

2 Arise, go to Nineveh, that great city, and cry against it; for their wickedness is come up before me.

3 But Jonah rose up to flee unto Tarshish from the presence of the Lord, and went down to Joppa; and he found a ship going to Tarshish: so he paid the fare thereof, and went down into it, to go with them unto Tarshish from the presence of the Lord.

4 But the Lord sent out a great wind into the sea, and there was a mighty tempest in the sea, so that the ship was like to be broken.

5 Then the mariners were afraid, and cried every man unto his god, and cast forth the wares that were in the ship into the sea, to lighten it of them. But Jonah was gone down into the sides of the ship; and he lay, and was fast asleep.

6 So the shipmaster came to him, and said unto him, What meanest thou, O sleeper? arise, call upon thy God, if so be that God will think upon us, that we perish not.

7 And they said every one to his fellow, Come, and let us cast lots, that we may know for whose cause this evil is upon us. So they cast lots, and the lot fell upon Jonah.

8 Then said they unto him, Tell us, we pray thee, for whose cause this evil is upon us; What is thine occupation? and whence comest thou? what is thy country? and of what people art thou?

9 And he said unto them, I am a Hebrew; and I fear the Lord, the God of heaven, which hath made the sea and the dry land.

10 Then were the men exceedingly afraid, and said unto him, Why hast thou done this? For the men knew that he fled from the presence of the Lord, because he had told them.

11 Then said they unto him, What shall we do unto thee, that the sea may be calm unto us? for the sea wrought, and was tempestuous.

12 And he said unto them, Take me up, and cast me forth into the sea; so shall the sea be calm unto you: for I know that for my sake this great tempest is upon you.

13 Nevertheless the men rowed hard to bring it to the land; but they could not: for the sea wrought, and was tempestuous against them.

14 Wherefore they cried unto the Lord, and said, We beseech thee,

O Lord, we beseech thee, let us not perish for this man's life, and lay not upon us innocent blood: for thou, O Lord, hast done as it pleased thee.

15 So they took up Jonah, and cast him forth into the sea: and the sea ceased from her raging.

16 Then the men feared the Lord exceedingly, and offered a sacrifice unto the Lord, and made vows.

17 Now the Lord had prepared a great fish to swallow up Jonah. And Jonah was in the belly of the fish three days and three nights.

CHAPTER 2

1 Then Jonah prayed unto the Lord his God out of the fish's belly,

2 And said, I cried by reason of mine affliction unto the Lord, and he heard me; out of the belly of hell cried I, and thou heardest my voice.

3 For thou hadst cast me into the deep, in the midst of the seas; and the floods compassed me about: all thy billows and thy waves passed over me.

4 Then I said, I am cast out of thy sight; yet I will look again toward thy holy temple.

5 The waters compassed me about, even to the soul: the depth closed me round about, the weeds were wrapped about my head.

6 I went down to the bottoms of the mountains; the earth with her bars was about me for ever: yet hast thou brought up my life from corruption, O Lord my God.

7 When my soul fainted within me I remembered the Lord: and my prayer came in unto thee, into thine holy temple.

8 They that observe lying vanities forsake their own mercy.

9 But I will sacrifice unto thee with the voice of thanksgiving; I will pay that that I have vowed. Salvation is of the Lord.

10 And the Lord spake unto the fish, and it vomited out Jonah upon the dry land.

CHAPTER 3

1 And the word of the Lord came unto Jonah the second time, saying,

2 Arise, go unto Nineveh, that great city, and preach unto it the preaching that I bid thee.

3 So Jonah arose, and went unto Nineveh, according to the word of the Lord. Now Nineveh was an exceeding great city of three days' journey.

4 And Jonah began to enter into the city a day's journey, and he cried, and said, Yet forty days, and Nineveh shall be overthrown.

5 So the people of Nineveh believed God, and proclaimed a fast, and put on sackcloth, from the greatest of them even to the least of them.

6 For word came unto the king of Nineveh, and he arose from his throne, and he laid his robe from him, and covered him with sackcloth, and sat in ashes.

7 And he caused it to be proclaimed and published through Nineveh by the decree of the king and his nobles, saying, Let neither man nor beast, herd nor flock, taste any thing: let them not feed, nor drink water:

8 But let man and beast be covered with sackcloth, and cry mightily unto God: yea, let them turn every one from his evil way, and from the violence that is in their hands.

9 Who can tell if God will turn and repent, and turn away from his fierce anger, that we perish not?

10 And God saw their works, that they turned from their evil way; and God repented of the evil, that he had said that he would do unto them; and he did it not.

CHAPTER 4

1 But it displeased Jonah exceedingly, and he was very angry.

2 And he prayed unto the Lord, and said, I pray thee, O Lord, was not this my saying, when I was yet in my country? Therefore I fled before

unto Tarshish: for I knew that thou art a gracious God, and merciful, slow to anger, and of great kindness, and repentest thee of the evil.

3 Therefore now, O Lord, take, I beseech thee, my life from me; for it is better for me to die than to live.

4 Then said the Lord, Doest thou well to be angry?

5 So Jonah went out of the city, and sat on the east side of the city, and there made him a booth, and sat under it in the shadow, till he might see what would become of the city.

6 And the Lord God prepared a gourd, and made it to come up over Jonah, that it might be a shadow over his head, to deliver him from his grief. So Jonah was exceedingly glad of the gourd.

7 But God prepared a worm when the morning rose the next day, and it smote the gourd that it withered.

8 And it came to pass, when the sun did arise, that God prepared a vehement east wind; and the sun beat upon the head of Jonah, that he fainted, and wished in himself to die, and said, It is better for me to die than to live.

9 And God said to Jonah, Doest thou well to be angry for the gourd? And he said, I do well to be angry, even unto death.

10 Then said the Lord, Thou hast had pity on the gourd, for the which thou hast not labored, neither madest it grow; which came up in a night, and perished in a night:

11 And should not I spare Nineveh, that great city, wherein are more than sixscore thousand persons that cannot discern between their right hand and their left hand; and also much cattle?

JONAH—CONDEMNATION OF EXCLUSIVENESS

A. The Prophet and His Times

I. *Dates.* Jonah was the son of Amittai (II Kings 14:25). There can be no doubt of identity, as these names occur nowhere else in the Old Testament. From these facts it is evident that Jonah prophesied about the time of the accession of Jeroboam II. This would make him, perhaps, an early contemporary with Hosea (Hosea 1:1) and Amos (Amos 1:1).

II. *Characteristics.* The relation of the Hebrew people to foreign nations, at this period was characterized by a strange contradiction: they were making alliances; and they were bitterly exclusive. Both these attitudes were wrong in the measure of their misinterpretation of the divine attitude, and prostitution of the divine purpose. Amos taught the sovereignty of Jehovah over all nations. Obadiah declared the judgment of God on an outside

nation which was disobedient as to the light it had. Jonah's story
was to teach the tenderness of God toward a repentant nation and
thus to rebuke the false exclusiveness of Israel.

B. The Analysis of the Prophecy

I. The first commission (chapters 1, 2).

a.   The prophet's commission and disobedience (1:1–3).
     1.   The commission (verses 1, 2).
          (a) The Word of the Lord.
          (b) Go to Nineveh—Cry against it.
          (c) For their wickedness.
     2.   The disobedience (verse 3).
          (a) Flight from the presence of the Lord (resignation of
               his office).
          (b) Ship at Joppa going to Tarshish (paid his fare).
b.   Jehovah's interposition (1:4–11).
     1.   The tempest.
          (a) The Lord sent out a wind.
          (b) The incidence of the storm.
     2.   Jonah cast out (verses 15–17).
          (a) The prophet cast out.
          (b) The prepared fish. Men can build a submarine boat
               to carry a hundred passengers, but they deny the
               great God the power to prepare a fish to carry one.
     3.   The experience of the deep (2:1, 2).
          (a) The fact stated. Prayed unto the Lord his God out
               of the new circumstances.
          (b) The tone of the praying. Quotations from the Psalms
               with more or less of literalness. The natural cry from
               one familiar with these Psalms.
     4.   The deliverance (verse 10). The Lord spake unto the fish
          and it vomited out Jonah.

II. The second commission (chapters 3, 4).

a.   The prophet's commission and obedience (chapter 3).
     1.   The commission.

(a) The Word of the Lord—second time.

(b) Go to Nineveh.

(c) "Preach the preaching I bid thee."

2. The obedience.

(a) Jonah arose, went, according to Word.

(b) Nineveh. Exceeding great.

(c) The preaching. (1) A day's journey. (2) "Yet forty days."

3. The result.

(a) The people believed God.

(b) Proclaimed a fast and repentance.

(c) God repented.

b. The prophet and Jehovah (chapter 4).

1. Jonah displeased (verses 1–3).

(a) Angry.

(b) Jonah's knowledge of Jehovah.

(c) Objected to exercise of mercy to outsiders.

(d) "Take my life"—self-centered.

2. Jehovah (verses 4–8).

(a) His question. "Doest thou well?"

(b) His gourd—prepared.

(c) His worm—prepared.

(d) His east wind—prepared.

3. Jonah distressed. Sun beat on his head; fainted; asked for death.

4. Jehovah (verses 9–11).

(a) His question.

(b) Jonah's answer. Thus at the end the prophet was out of harmony with God.

(c) Jehovah's vindication of himself.

The Message of Jonah

This is a prophetic story. The prophet's experiences are intended to teach the chosen people the lesson of the inclusiveness of the divine government, and to rebuke the exclusiveness of their attitude. Thus it was also a prophecy of the supreme proof of these things which came in the person and mission of Jesus: His death, His resurrection, His going forth to all nations. Thus at the last in his persistent displeasure, Jonah represents the nation in its ultimate failure to symphathize with God.

C. THE PERMANENT MESSAGE

I. *Stated.* The first message of the story is that we ought ever to be ready to form our ideas by the acts of God, rather than interpret His acts by our prejudices. Jonah attempted to interpret the activity of God by the prejudice and conviction of his heart. There are times when we must be ready to give up prejudice and conviction and to say in the presence of an act of God, "That is right, though I cannot trace its meaning." Jonah had not learned that lesson.

Again let me emphasize, for Christian workers especially, this simple lesson. The fact that there was a ship ready at Joppa, though a favorable circumstance, and the act of paying the fare, though there was a fine touch of independence about it, did not warrant him in expecting to reach Tarshish if God wanted him in Nineveh.

The exclusiveness which would exclude any from the covenant of grace is utterly opposed to the purpose of Jehovah. God is no respecter of persons. He is a respecter of character. We have hardly begun to learn that lesson in the Church up to this moment; we are still exclusive with an exclusiveness that dishonors God.

II. *The Application.* The story has an application of special urgency for the Holy Nation which is created by way of the death and resurrection of Jesus. Our understanding of and identification with His death and His resurrection is measured, not by our ability to state it in theological formulas, or by our ability to preach its doctrines, but our appreciation or apprehension of the truth concerning the death and the resurrection of Jesus is measured by our readiness to carry the message of the divine compassion and love to all the sinning nations; by our readiness to go to Nineveh and preach, and when Nineveh repents to rejoice with God over that repentance. That is the only proof of our true understanding of the sign of Jonah as fulfilled in the history and marvelous work of the Son of Man. O brethren, how much of the attitude of Jonah is among us, without his honesty!

Now will you not take your Bible and begin to preach it? How many have preached on this book of Jonah recently? I will suggest a series of sermons on the book of Jonah. Never mind the fish. Men have been looking so hard at the great fish that they have failed to see the great God. Oh, in God's name, look above the fish and see what truth lies behind. I would like to preach a series of six sermons on the book of Jonah.

1. First, I would read the book of Jonah. We do not have enough of that kind of thing. Men give dramatic recitals of Shakespeare. Why can we not take this book, not to dramatize it so as to show the ability of the dramatist, but read it to give the sense? I would read it for one sermon, making such annotations and explanations of the text as would illuminate it.

2. Next I would preach on "The Governing God." You will find it on every page.

3. Next I would preach on "The Longsuffering God"; long-suffering with a nation, longsuffering with a man.

4. For another subject I would preach on "National Account-ability"; the perishing or permanent element in a nation depends upon a nation's relationship to God, whether it is Israel or Nineveh.

5. Then I would preach on "Personal Responsibility" as evidenced in the life story of Jonah.

6. I would take one more Sunday morning for a sermon on "How to Cooperate with God" in accomplishing God's work. Try Jonah, my brother, and let Browning rest a little.

CHAPTER 6

MICAH

CHAPTER 1

1 The word of the Lord that came to Micah the Morasthite in the days of Jotham, Ahaz, and Hezekiah, kings of Judah, which he saw concerning Samaria and Jerusalem.

2 Hear, all ye people; hearken, O earth, and all that therein is: and let the Lord God be witness against you, the Lord from his holy temple.

3 For, behold, the Lord cometh forth out of his place, and will come down, and tread upon the high places of the earth.

4 And the mountains shall be molten under him, and the valleys shall be cleft, as wax before the fire, and as the waters that are poured down a steep place.

5 For the transgression of Jacob is all this, and for the sins of the house of Israel. What is the transgression of Jacob? is it not Samaria? and what are the high places of Judah? are they not Jerusalem?

6 Prophesy ye not, say they to a heap of the field, and as plantings of a vineyard: and I will pour down the stones thereof into the valley, and I will discover the foundations thereof.

7 And all the graven images thereof shall be beaten to pieces, and all the hires thereof shall be burned with the fire, and all the idols thereof will I lay desolate: for she gathered it of the hire of a harlot, and they shall return to the hire of a harlot.

8 Therefore I will wail and howl, I will go stripped and naked: I will make a wailing like the dragons, and mourning as the owls.

9 For her wound is incurable; for it is come unto Judah; he is come unto the gate of my people, even to Jerusalem.

10 Declare ye it not at Gath, weep ye not at all: in the house of Aphrah roll thyself in the dust.

11 Pass ye away, thou inhabitant of Saphir, having thy shame naked: the inhabitant of Zaanan came not forth in the mourning of Bethezel; he shall receive of you his standing.

12 For the inhabitant of Maroth waited carefully for good: but evil came down from the Lord unto the gate of Jerusalem.

13 O thou inhabitant of Lachish, bind the chariot to the swift beast: she is the beginning of the sin to the daughter of Zion: for the transgressions of Israel were found in thee.

14 Therefore shalt thou give pres-

70

ents to Moreshethgath: the houses of Achzib shall be a lie to the kings of Israel.

15 Yet will I bring an heir unto thee, O inhabitant of Mareshah: he shall come unto Adullam the glory of Israel.

16 Make thee bald, and poll thee for thy delicate children; enlarge thy baldness as the eagle; for they are gone into captivity from thee.

CHAPTER 2

1 Woe to them that devise iniquity, and work evil upon their beds! when the morning is light, they practise it, because it is in the power of their hand.

2 And they covet fields, and take them by violence; and houses, and take them away: so they oppress a man and his house, even a man and his heritage.

3 Therefore thus saith the Lord; Behold, against this family do I devise an evil, from which ye shall not remove your necks; neither shall ye go haughtily: for this time is evil.

4 In that day shall one take up a parable against you, and lament with a doleful lamentation, and say, We be utterly spoiled: he hath changed the portion of my people: how hath he removed it from me! turning away he hath divided our fields.

5 Therefore thou shalt have none that shall cast a cord by lot in the congregation of the Lord.

6 Prophesy ye not, say they to them that prophesy: they shall not prophesy to them, that they shall not take shame.

7 O thou that art named the house of Jacob, is the Spirit of the Lord straitened? are these his doings? do not my words do good to him that walketh uprightly?

8 Even of late my people is risen up as an enemy: ye pull off the robe with the garment from them that pass by securely as men averse from war.

9 The women of my people have

ye cast out from their pleasant houses; from their children have ye taken away my glory for ever.

10 Arise ye, and depart; for this is not your rest: because it is polluted, it shall destroy you, even with a sore destruction.

11 If a man walking in the spirit and falsehood do lie, saying, I will prophesy unto thee of wine and of strong drink; he shall even be the prophet of this people.

12 I will surely assemble, O Jacob, all of thee; I will surely gather the remnant of Israel; I will put them together as the sheep of Bozrah, as the flock in the midst of their fold: they shall make great noise by reason of the multitude of men.

13 The breaker is come up before them: they have broken up, and have passed through the gate, and are gone out by it; and their king shall pass before them, and the Lord on the head of them.

CHAPTER 3

1 And I said, Hear, I pray you, O heads of Jacob, and ye princes of the house of Israel; Is it not for you to know judgment?

2 Who hate the good, and love the evil; who pluck off their skin from off them, and their flesh from off their bones;

3 Who also eat the flesh of my people, and flay their skin from off them; and they break their bones, and chop them in pieces, as for the pot, and as flesh within the caldron.

4 Then shall they cry unto the Lord, but he will not hear them: he will even hide his face from them at that time, as they have behaved themselves ill in their doings.

5 Thus saith the Lord concerning the prophets that make my people err, that bite with their teeth, and cry, Peace; and he that putteth not into their mouths, they even prepare war against him:

6 Therefore night shall be unto

you, that ye shall not have a vision; and it shall be dark unto you, that ye shall not divine; and the sun shall go down over the prophets, and the day shall be dark over them.

7 Then shall the seers be ashamed, and the diviners confounded: yea, they shall all cover their lips; for there is no answer of God.

8 But truly I am full of power by the Spirit of the Lord, and of judgment, and of might, to declare unto Jacob his transgression, and to Israel his sin.

9 Hear this, I pray you, ye heads of the house of Jacob, and princes of the house of Israel, that abhor judgment, and pervert all equity.

10 They build up Zion with blood, and Jerusalem with iniquity.

11 The heads thereof judge for reward, and the priests thereof teach for hire, and the prophets thereof divine for money: yet will they lean upon the Lord, and say, Is not the Lord among us? none evil can come upon us.

12 Therefore shall Zion for your sake be plowed as a field, and Jerusalem shall become heaps, and the mountain of the house as the high places of the forest.

CHAPTER 4

1 But in the last days it shall come to pass, that the mountain of the house of the Lord shall be established in the top of the mountains, and it shall be exalted above the hills; and people shall flow unto it.

2 And many nations shall come, and say, Come, and let us go up to the mountain of the Lord, and to the house of the God of Jacob; and he will teach us of his ways, and we will walk in his paths: for the law shall go forth of Zion, and the word of the Lord from Jerusalem.

3 And he shall judge among many people, and rebuke strong nations afar off; and they shall beat their swords into plowshares, and their spears into pruning hooks: nation shall not lift up a sword against nation, neither shall they learn war any more.

4 But they shall sit every man under his vine and under his fig tree; and none shall make them afraid: for the mouth of the Lord of hosts hath spoken it.

5 For all people will walk every one in the name of his god, and we will walk in the name of the Lord our God for ever and ever.

6 In that day, saith the Lord, will I assemble her that halteth, and I will gather her that is driven out, and her that I have afflicted;

7 And I will make her that halted a remnant, and her that was cast far off a strong nation: and the Lord shall reign over them in mount Zion from henceforth, even for ever.

8 And thou, O tower of the flock, the stronghold of the daughter of Zion, unto thee shall it come, even the first dominion; the kingdom shall come to the daughter of Jerusalem.

9 Now why dost thou cry out aloud? is there no king in thee? is thy counselor perished? for pangs have taken thee as a woman in travail.

10 Be in pain, and labor to bring forth, O daughter of Zion, like a woman in travail: for now shalt thou go forth out of the city, and thou shalt dwell in the field, and thou shalt go even to Babylon; there shalt thou be delivered; there the Lord shall redeem thee from the hand of thine enemies.

11 Now also many nations are gathered against thee, that say, Let her be defiled, and let our eye look upon Zion.

12 But they know not the thoughts of the Lord, neither understand they his counsel: for he shall gather them as the sheaves into the floor.

13 Arise and thresh, O daughter of Zion; for I will make thine horn iron, and I will make thy hoofs brass: and thou shalt beat in pieces many peo-

ple: and I will consecrate their gain unto the Lord, and their substance unto the Lord of the whole earth.

CHAPTER 5

1 Now gather thyself in troops, O daughter of troops: he hath laid siege against us: they shall smite the judge of Israel with a rod upon the cheek.

2 But thou, Bethlehem Ephratah, though thou be little among the thousands of Judah, yet out of thee shall he come forth unto me that is to be ruler in Israel; whose goings forth have been from of old, from everlasting.

3 Therefore will he give them up, until the time that she which travaileth hath brought forth: then the remnant of his brethren shall return unto the children of Israel.

4 And he shall stand and feed in the strength of the Lord, in the majesty of the name of the Lord his God; and they shall abide: for now shall he be great unto the ends of the earth.

5 And this man shall be the peace, when the Assyrian shall come into our land: and when he shall tread in our palaces, then shall we raise against him seven shepherds, and eight principal men.

6 And they shall waste the land of Assyria with the sword, and the land of Nimrod in the entrances thereof: thus shall he deliver us from the Assyrian, when he cometh into our land, and when he treadeth within our borders.

7 And the remnant of Jacob shall be in the midst of many people as a dew from the Lord, as the showers upon the grass, that tarrieth not for man, nor waiteth for the sons of men.

8 And the remnant of Jacob shall be among the Gentiles in the midst of many people, as a lion among the beasts of the forest, as a young lion among the flocks of sheep: who, if he go through, both treadeth down,

and teareth in pieces, and none can deliver.

9 Thine hand shall be lifted up upon thine adversaries, and all thine enemies shall be cut off.

10 And it shall come to pass in that day, saith the Lord, that I will cut off thy horses out of the midst of thee, and I will destroy thy chariots:

11 And I will cut off the cities of thy land, and throw down all thy strongholds:

12 And I will cut off witchcrafts out of thine hand; and thou shalt have no more soothsayers:

13 Thy graven images also will I cut off, and thy standing images out of the midst of thee; and thou shalt no more worship the work of thine hands.

14 And I will pluck up thy groves out of the midst of thee: so will I destroy thy cities.

15 And I will execute vengeance in anger and fury upon the heathen, such as they have not heard.

CHAPTER 6

1 Hear ye now what the Lord saith; Arise, contend thou before the mountains, and let the hills hear thy voice.

2 Hear ye, O mountains, the Lord's controversy, and ye strong foundations of the earth: for the Lord hath a controversy with his people, and he will plead with Israel.

3 O my people, what have I done unto thee? and wherein have I wearied thee? testify against me.

4 For I brought thee up out of the land of Egypt, and redeemed thee out of the house of servants; and I sent before thee Moses, Aaron, and Miriam.

5 O my people, remember now what Balak king of Moab consulted, and what Balaam the son of Beor answered him from Shittim unto Gilgal; that ye may know the righteousness of the Lord.

6 Wherewith shall I come before

the Lord, and bow myself before the high God? shall I come before him with burnt offerings, with calves of a year old?

7 Will the Lord be pleased with thousands of rams, or with ten thousands of rivers of oil? shall I give my firstborn for my transgression, the fruit of my body for the sin of my soul?

8 He hath showed thee, O man, what is good; and what doth the Lord require of thee, but to do justly, and to love mercy, and to walk humbly with thy God?

9 The Lord's voice crieth unto the city, and the man of wisdom shall see thy name: hear ye the rod, and who hath appointed it.

10 Are there yet the treasures of wickedness in the house of the wicked, and the scant measure that is abominable?

11 Shall I count them pure with the wicked balances, and with the bag of deceitful weights?

12 For the rich men thereof are full of violence, and the inhabitants thereof have spoken lies, and their tongue is deceitful in their mouth.

13 Therefore also will I make thee sick in smiting thee, in making thee desolate because of thy sins.

14 Thou shalt eat, but not be satisfied; and thy casting down shall be in the midst of thee; and thou shalt take hold, but shalt not deliver; and that which thou deliverest will I give up to the sword.

15 Thou shalt sow, but thou shalt not reap; thou shalt tread the olives, but thou shalt not anoint thee with oil; and sweet wine, but shalt not drink wine.

16 For the statutes of Omri are kept, and all the works of the house of Ahab, and ye walk in their counsels; that I should make thee a desolation, and the inhabitants thereof a hissing: therefore ye shall bear the reproach of my people.

CHAPTER 7

1 Woe is me! for I am as when they have gathered the summer fruits, as the grape gleanings of the vintage: there is no cluster to eat: my soul desired the first ripe fruit.

2 The good man is perished out of the earth; and there is none upright among men: they all lie in wait for blood; they hunt every man his brother with a net.

3 That they may do evil with both hands earnestly, the prince asketh, and the judge asketh for a reward; and the great man, he uttereth his mischievous desire: so they wrap it up.

4 The best of them is as a brier: the most upright is sharper than a thorn hedge: the day of thy watchmen and thy visitation cometh; now shall be their perplexity.

5 Trust ye not in a friend, put ye not confidence in a guide: keep the doors of thy mouth from her that lieth in thy bosom.

6 For the son dishonoreth the father, the daughter riseth up against her mother, the daughter-in-law against her mother-in-law: a man's enemies are the men of his own house.

7 Therefore I will look unto the Lord; I will wait for the God of my salvation: my God will hear me.

8 Rejoice not against me, O mine enemy: when I fall, I shall arise; when I sit in darkness, the Lord shall be a light unto me.

9 I will bear the indignation of the Lord, because I have sinned against him, until he plead my cause, and execute judgment for me: he will bring me forth to the light, and I shall behold his righteousness.

10 Then she that is mine enemy shall see it, and shame shall cover her which said unto me, Where is the Lord thy God? mine eyes shall behold her: now shall she be trodden down as the mire of the streets.

11 In the day that thy walls are

to be built, in that day shall the decree be far removed.

12 In that day also he shall come even to thee from Assyria, and from the fortified cities, and from the fortress even to the river, and from sea to sea, and from mountain to mountain.

13 Notwithstanding, the land shall be desolate because of them that dwell therein, for the fruit of their doings.

14 Feed thy people with thy rod, the flock of thine heritage, which dwell solitarily in the wood, in the midst of Carmel: let them feed in Bashan and Gilead, as in the days of old.

15 According to the days of thy coming out of the land of Egypt will I show unto him marvelous things.

16 The nations shall see and be confounded at all their might: they shall lay their hand upon their mouth, their ears shall be deaf.

17 They shall lick the dust like a serpent, they shall move out of their holes like worms of the earth: they shall be afraid of the Lord our God, and shall fear because of thee.

18 Who is a God like unto thee, that pardoneth iniquity, and passeth by the transgression of the remnant of his heritage? he retaineth not his anger for ever, because he delighteth in mercy.

19 He will turn again, he will have compassion upon us; he will subdue our iniquities; and thou wilt cast all their sins into the depths of the sea.

20 Thou will perform the truth to Jacob, and the mercy to Abraham, which thou hast sworn unto our fathers from the days of old.

MICAH—AUTHORITY, TRUE AND FALSE

A. THE PROPHET AND HIS TIMES

I. *Dates.* Micah prophesied in the early part of the reign of King Hezekiah (Jeremiah 26:17–19). He was contemporary with Isaiah, who prophesied during part of Uzziah's reign, and who was in the zenith of his power when Hezekiah had been reigning eighteen years. Micah began after Uzziah's death, and must have ended in the early part of Hezekiah's reign, for the idolatries he rebuked were done away with at Hezekiah's reformation. A comparison of these dates with those introducing Hosea's prophecy will show that this aged prophet was still speaking during Micah's period.

II. *Characteristics.* The message of Micah wa speculiarly to the cities of Israel and Judah as the centers affecting the national thought and action (Micah 1:1). The sins he rebukes are peculiarly those of cities: Oppression and violence, corruption of princes, prophets and priests, bribery, robbery, dishonesty, pride. The prophecy is a declaration of a devine program. It consists of three addresses, each beginning with a call to hear (1:2, 3:1; 6:1). The prophet declares to those in authority, in the centers of authority, the messages of Him who is supreme.

B. The Analysis of the Prophecy

I. *A message to the nations concerning the chosen (chapters 1, 2).*

a. The summons (1:2–4).
    1. To all people. The prophet here has clearly in mind the attitude of Jehovah toward the whole earth. Israel is His medium of teaching, if not in blessing, then in judgment. Jehovah witnesses among the nations by His dealings with Israel.
    2. Jehovah's coming.
        (a) From His place—heaven where is His throne, and where His Kingdom is perfect.
        (b) To the earth—where men have rebelled. To the high places of His rebellious authority.
        (c) The storm—under the figure of a great upheaval of nature, the prophet describes the advent of God.
b. Declamation of Jehovah (1:5–7).
    1. The cause of judgment declared (verse 5).
        (a) Stated: (1) "For the transgression of Jacob." (2) "For the sins of the house of Israel."
        (b) Explained: (1) "Is it not Samaria?" (2) "Are they not Jerusalem?"
The reason of the judgment is declared to be the apostasy of the whole nation, as they are evident in the cities.
    2. The course of judgment announced (verses 6, 7).
        (a) The destruction of the city (verse 6).
        (b) The destruction of the false religion (verse 7).
The city, where was gathered the wealth and where was ex-

ercised the authority. was to be demolished, and the religion of
apostasy was to be swept out.

c. The prophetic message (1:8–2:5).
    1. Lamentation of the prophet (1:8–10).
        (a) Personal grief.
        (b) The wounds of the people incurable.
        (c) "Tell it not in Gath . . . weep not at all."
    2. A wailing description of the judgment (verses 11–16).
        Here follows a series of paronomasias. The passage is a
        strange mixture of grief and satire. At the calamity he is
        grieved; at the sin he is angry. This merging of agony and
        anger flashes into satire. The connection or contrast is not
        always easy to discover.
        Beth-le-aphrah—house of dust.
        Saphir—beautiful.
        Zaanan—sheep pastures.
        Beth-ezel—house of the tide.
        Maroth—bitter springs.
        Lachish—Rechesh-Swiftbeast.
        Moresheth-Gath—possession of Gath.
        Achzib Deceitful—brook failing in summer.
        Mareshah—summit.
A reading of the section with the translation will give a faint
idea of the weird effect of this lamentation. The play on words
is as though we said, "In Philadelphia there is no 'brotherly love.'"
    3. The cause stated (2:1–5).
        (a) The sin (verses 1, 2).
        (b) The consequent action of Jehovah (verse 3).
        (c) The mockery of observers who imitate their sorrow.
        (d) Utter dispossession (verse 5).

d. The false prophets.
    1. They interrupt the prophet and protest against his mes-
        sage, basing their objection upon the goodness of God.
    2. To them Jehovah's answer is that the changed and re-
        bellious attitude of His people accounts for the change in
        His attitude.
    3. Micah's keen satire.

e. The promise of deliverance (verses 12, 13). The first message

in the hearing of the nations closes with words spoken to
Jacob. It is an undefined promise of deliverance yet to come.

II. *A message to rulers concerning the coming one*
(chapters 3—5).

a. The sin of the heads and consequent judgment (3:1–12).
    1. The princes (verses 1–4).
       (a) The summons and declared requirements.
       (b) The charge: As to character—hate the good, etc.; as
           to conduct—spoil the people.
       (c) The judgment.
    2. The prophets (verses 5–8).
       (a) The son of the prophets. Make the people err. Fed—
           they cry peace; unfed—they make war.
       (b) The judgment: Retribution in kind; shame and un-
           cleanness.
       (c) Micah's defense by contrast.
    3. All the ruling classes (verses 9–12).
       (a) The charge: Heads—judge for reward; priests—
           teach for hire; prophets—divine for money.
       (b) Judgment: Zion—plowed as a field; Jerusalem—
           become heaps; The Mount—as high places of the
           forest.
b. The coming One and consequent deliverance (chapters 4, 5).
    1. The vision of restored order (4—5:1).
       (a) A look ahead (4:1–7). (1) The mountain—es-
           tablished; exalted; people shall flow. (2) Zion—
           the law; Jerusalem—the Word of the Lord. (3) the
           sequence—many nations; strong nations; no more
           war; peaceful possession.
       (b) The present in light of future (4:8—5:1). (1) As-
           surance. "It shall come." (2) Hope. "Why dost thou
           cry?" Is there no king? (3) Pains and deliverance
           foretold.
    2. The Deliverer and the deliverance (5:2–15).
       (a) The coming One (verse 2).
       (b) His program (verses 3–9).

    (c) The Word of Jehovah concerning it (verses 10–15). Destruction of all false strength and confidences.

III. A message to the chosen concerning the controversy (chapters 6, 7).

Note. This closing section is dramatic and magnificent. The prophet summons Israel, and the mountains also, to hear the controversy. The key word is "Jehovah will plead." Then follows the controversy in which Jehovah, the prophet and the people take part.

a. The prophet (6:1, 2). The summons.
b. Jehovah (verses 3–5). A plaintive appeal.
c. The people (verses 6, 7). The questions of conviction.
d. The prophet (verses 8, 9). The answer.
e. Jehovah (verses 10–16). A terrible charge.
f. The people (7:1–10). Confession and hope.
g. The prophet (verses 11–13). The answer of hope.
h. The people (verse 14). At prayer.
i. Jehovah (verse 15). The answer of peace.
j. The prophet (verses 16, 17). Faith expressing the promise.
k. The people (verses 18–20). The final doxology.

THE MESSAGE OF MICAH

The message of Micah centers around the subject of authority. The prophet arraigned and condemned the false authority of those who had departed from the true standards of government, whether princes, prophets, or priests. This the prophet did by showing the influence of prostituted power and the judgments which resulted: "Zion—ploughed; Jerusalem—heaps; the mountain—the high places of a forest." The hope of the nation, according to this prophecy, was in the coming of a Ruler to Israel. The great central statement of the prophecy is this, "This man shall be our peace," and the restoration of order that would follow the coming ruler: the mountain of the Lord's house established; from Zion, instruction going forth; from Jerusalem, the Word of the Lord. Then the nations around would flow in and share in the blessing. In His establishment all false confidences are to be destroyed (5:10–15).

C. The Permanent Message

I. *Stated.* The permanent message of the prophecy is the message that the prophet delivered to his own day. The supreme authority in all the affairs of men is God. All human authority is subservient to the divine. The powers that be are ordained of God. In proportion as earth's rulers recognize this, they rule for the well-being of the people. Wherein they fail, the people are corrupted and depraved. Rulers who judge for reward, priests who teach for hire, and prophets who divine for money, are abhorrent to God and will be judged by Him. The one hope of a perfect system of government is that of the coming of God's own King. He came to lay foundations; He will come again to bring on the top stone. There is nothing the world wants today so much as a perfect system of government. The world is trying to find it in all directions: absolute monarchy, and limited monarchy and republican institutions. All the world over men are trying to find the perfect system, but there is only one perfect system, and that is the absolute monarchy of God Almighty in Jesus Christ. The world will never find its true order and its true peace until all other governors—whether emperors, kings, or presidents—have kissed the sceptre of the King of kings and reign under His control. That is the great message of Micah.

II. *Applied.* The application of this message can be stated in a few sentences. The Holy Nation—the Church, as Peter describes her—stands in the world for the recognition and enforcement of these great truths. There is to be among them, first, a realization of, and testimony to, the divine kingship. There is, moreover, to be a clear understanding that what the world needs is a true system of government, and that it can never come save through God's crowned and anointed King. Yet the whole nation is to exert its influence perpetually among men to enforce the recognition of God nationally, socially and municipally.

We stand as an influence in the nation for the throne of God, and whether in the government of the city or nation we must make our voice heard and influence felt. We do not believe in God if we are indifferent in the presence of the sins and corruptions that are cursing our cities. At last the King will set these things in order, but while He is hidden He can only be known through us, and we have no right to live in any township or any city in which the township and city does not come to know that we stand for the throne of God, and for the establishment of righteousness, and for the preëminence of Jesus Christ.

May God, in His great love and grace, drive us from these studies into a closer study of this great library of God so full of truth, that grips the conscience now just as it did in olden times; and may we, learning what the Word says, pass infinitely beyond that into the doing of what it says, that we may show forth His praise not only with our lips, but in our lives.

CHAPTER 7

NAHUM

1 The burden of Nineveh. The book of the vision of Nahum the Elkoshite.

2 God is jealous, and the Lord revengeth; the Lord revengeth, and is furious; the Lord will take vengeance on his adversaries, and he reserveth wrath for his enemies.

3 The Lord is slow to anger, and great in power, and will not at all acquit the wicked: the Lord hath his way in the whirlwind and in the storm, and the clouds are the dust of his feet.

4 He rebuketh the sea, and maketh it dry, and drieth up all the rivers: Bashan languisheth, and Carmel, and the flower of Lebanon languisheth.

5 The mountains quake at him, and the hills melt, and the earth is burned at his presence, yea, the world, and all that dwell therein.

6 Who can stand before his indignation? and who can abide in the fierceness of his anger? his fury is poured out like fire, and the rocks are thrown down by him.

7 The Lord is good, a stronghold in the day of trouble; and he knoweth them that trust in him.

8 But with an overrunning flood he will make an utter end of the place thereof, and darkness shall pursue his enemies.

9 What do ye imagine against the Lord? he will make an utter end: affliction shall not rise up the second time.

10 For while they be folden together as thorns, and while they are drunken as drunkards, they shall be devoured as stubble fully dry.

11 There is one come out of thee, that imagineth evil against the Lord, a wicked counselor.

12 Thus saith the Lord; Though they be quiet, and likewise many, yet thus shall they be cut down, when he shall pass through. Though I have afflicted thee, I will afflict thee no more.

13 For now will I break his yoke from off thee, and will burst thy bonds in sunder.

14 And the Lord hath given a commandment concerning thee, that no more of thy name be sown: out of the house of thy gods will I cut off the graven image and the molten image: I will make thy grave; for thou art vile.

15 Behold upon the mountains the feet of him that bringeth good tidings, that publisheth peace. O Judah, keep thy solemn feasts, per-

form thy vows: for the wicked shall no more pass through thee; he is utterly cut off.

CHAPTER 2

1 He that dasheth in pieces is come up before thy face: keep the munition, watch the way, make thy loins strong, fortify thy power mightily.

2 For the Lord hath turned away the excellency of Jacob, as the excellency of Israel: for the emptiers have emptied them out, and marred their vine branches.

3 The shield of his mighty men is made red, the valiant men are in scarlet: the chariots shall be with flaming torches in the day of his preparation, and the fir trees shall be terribly shaken.

4 The chariots shall rage in the streets, they shall justle one against another in the broad ways: they shall seem like torches, they shall run like the lightnings.

5 He shall recount his worthies: they shall stumble in their walk; they shall make haste to the wall thereof, and the defense shall be prepared.

6 The gates of the rivers shall be opened, and the palace shall be dissolved.

7 And Huzzab shall be led away captive, she shall be brought up, and her maids shall lead her as with the voice of doves, taboring upon their breasts.

8 But Nineveh is of old like a pool of water: yet they shall flee away. Stand, stand, shall they cry; but none shall look back.

9 Take ye the spoil of silver, take the spoil of gold: for there is none end of the store and glory out of all the pleasant furniture.

10 She is empty, and void, and waste: and the heart melteth, and the knees smite together, and much pain is in all loins, and the faces of them all gather blackness.

11 Where is the dwelling of the lions, and the feeding place of the young lions, where the lion, even the old lion, walked, and the lion's whelp, and none made them afraid?

12 The lion did tear in pieces enough for his whelps, and strangled for his lionesses, and filled his holes with prey, and his dens with ravin.

13 Behold, I am against thee, saith the Lord of hosts, and I will burn her chariots in the smoke, and the sword shall devour thy young lions: and I will cut off thy prey from the earth, and the voice of thy messengers shall no more be heard.

CHAPTER 3

1 Woe to the bloody city! it is all full of lies and robbery; the prey departeth not;

2 The noise of a whip, and the noise of the rattling of the wheels, and of the prancing horses, and of the jumping chariots.

3 The horseman lifteth up both the bright sword and the glittering spear: and there is a multitude of slain, and a great number of carcasses; and there is none end of their corpses; they stumble upon their corpses:

4 Because of the multitude of the whoredoms of the well-favored harlot, the mistress of witchcrafts, that selleth nations through her whoredoms, and families through her witchcrafts.

5 Behold, I am against thee, saith the Lord of hosts; and I will discover thy skirts upon thy face, and I will show the nations thy nakedness, and the kingdoms thy shame.

6 And I will cast abominable filth upon thee, and make thee vile, and will set thee as a gazingstock.

7 And it shall come to pass, that all they that look upon thee shall flee from thee, and say, Nineveh is laid waste: who will bemoan her? whence shall I seek comforters for thee?

8 Art thou better than populous No, that was situate among the rivers, that had the waters round about it,

whose rampart was the sea, and her wall was from the sea?

9 Ethiopia and Egypt were her strength, and it was infinite; Put and Lubim were thy helpers.

10 Yet was she carried away, she went into captivity: her young children also were dashed in pieces at the top of all the streets: and they cast lots for her honorable men, and all her great men were bound in chains.

11 Thou also shalt be drunken: thou shalt be hid, thou also shalt seek strength because of the enemy.

12 All thy strongholds shall be like fig trees with the first ripe figs: if they be shaken, they shall even fall into the mouth of the eater.

13 Behold, thy people in the midst of thee are women: the gates of thy land shall be set wide open unto thine enemies: the fire shall devour thy bars.

14 Draw thee waters for the siege, fortify thy strongholds: go into clay, and tread the mortar, make strong the brickkiln.

15 There shall the fire devour thee; the sword shall cut thee off, it shall eat thee up like the cankerworm: make thyself many as the cankerworm, make thyself many as the locusts.

16 Thou hast multiplied thy merchants above the stars of heaven: the cankerworm spoileth, and fleeth away.

17 Thy crowned are as the locusts, and thy captains as the great grasshoppers, which camp in the hedges in the cold day, but when the sun ariseth they flee away, and their place is not known where they are.

18 Thy shepherds slumber, O king of Assyria: thy nobles shall dwell in the dust: thy people is scattered upon the mountains, and no man gathereth them.

19 There is no healing of thy bruise; thy wound is grievous: all that hear the bruit of thee shall clap the hands over thee: for upon whom hath not thy wickedness passed continually?

NAHUM—THE VINDICATION OF VENGEANCE

A. THE PROPHET AND HIS TIMES

I. *Dates.* Nothing more is known of the prophet than is declared in the title. He was a native of Elkosh, but this town cannot be located with certainty. Some place it in Assyria, and defend this by the traditions, and by his evident acquaintance with local terms such as Huzzab (2:7). Some place it in Palestine, and quote his references to Lebanon, Carmel and Bashan. The location is uncertain and unimportant.

The date must have been at any rate after the fall of Thebes, B.C. 663 (see 3:8, where "No-Amon" refers to Thebes) and before the fall of Nineveh, B.C. 606. This is sufficiently definite, and there is practical unanimity.

There is a suggestiveness in the meaning of the prophet's name, "Nahum," which signifies, "the full of exceeding comfort."

II. *Characteristics.* The Northern Kingdom at the time of the prophecy had been destroyed, and the ten tribes were dispersed. The prophet's message was to Judah and it was delivered almost certainly during those days succeeding Hezekiah's reign and very probably in close connection with Manasseh's return from captivity. The Assyrian power seems to be at its very height. The descriptions are those of arrogance and oppression. Nahum is not sent to Nineveh as Jonah was. The time for such opportunity is passed. He declares to Judah the coming overthrow of their enemy. It is the message of the "full end" (1:8, 9).

B. THE ANALYSIS OF THE PROPHECY

I. *The verdict of vengeance (chapter 1).*

a. The subject and the method (verse 1).
    1. The burden of Nineveh.
    2. Vision of Nahum.
b. Jehovah (1:2–8). His conduct must harmonize with His character.
    1. Declaration of His character (verses 2, 3).
       (a) Main subject: His vengence, Reason—"A jealous God"; Action—"Avengeth"; Objects—"His adversaries."
       (b) The central fact: "Slow to anger."
    2. Revelation of His majesty (verses 4–6).
       (a) The storm symbol—hurricane for the sea; simoon for the land.
       (b) The question emphasizing the resistless force of His might.
    3. Affirmation of His method (verses 7, 8).
       (a) To His friends—"Good . . . a stronghold" (verse 7).
       (b) To His foes—"make a full end" (verse 8).
c. The verdict (1:9–14).
    1. Addressed toward Nineveh (verses 9–11).
       (a) The question (verse 9): Hinting at the final sin. Setting it in the light of Jehovah. (Emphasize "Ye" and "Jehovah.")

     (b) The announcement of judgment (verses 9, 10): "A full end." "Affliction" (Jonah 3:5-9). The weakness of defense.

     (c) The central charge (verse 11). Devising evil against Jehovah. (Compare Isaiah 36:18-20.)

  2. Addressed to Israel (verses 12, 13). As other prophets have summoned nations to attend to God's controversy with Israel, so now Israel is addressed with regard to Nineveh's doom.

  3. Addressed to Nineveh (verse 14).

     (a) The sentence: "I will make thy grave."

     (b) The reason: "Thou art vile."

d. The cry to Judah (verse 15). The verdict of vengeance to Nineveh is the publication of an evangel to Judah.

     (a) Good tidings: Deliverance brings peace.

     (b) Responsibility: Keep thy fast; perform thy vows.

II. The vision of vengeance (chapter 2).

a. Preliminary declaration (2:1, 2).

  1. The advent of the avenger (verse 1).

     (a) The fact announced. The Disperser. (Literally "The Hammer," the reference being to the instrument, but there is a recognition of the hand which wields the "Hammer.")

     (b) Ironical advice to prepare.

  2. Purpose of the vengeance. Restoration. Note: "The excellency of Jacob as the excellency of Israel."

b. The vision (2:3-10).

  1. The conflict (verses 3-5). Interpretations of the details greatly differ. I give that which, to my mind, most accurately meets all the facts of the case.

     (a) The attacking army (verse 3).

     (b) The defending army (verse 4).

     (c) The battle: Defense and attack (verse 5).

  2. The conquest (verses 6-9).

     (a) The flood (verse 6). The act of God.

Note. Diodorus Seculus mentions an old prophecy that the city would never be taken until the river should become its enemy. He

declares that during the enemy's attack the river burst its banks
and washed away the wall for twenty stadia (2¼ miles).

        (b) The capture (verse 7). "It is decreed." Reference to
            the flood as determined by God. The city under the
            figure of a woman and her attendants.
        (c) Flight of the multitudes (verse 8).
        (d) Sack of the city (verse 9).
    3. The consummation (verse 10).
        (a) Nineveh: "Empty . . . Hollow." "Void . . . Waste."
        (b) The people. "Heart": Failure of inward courage.
            "Knees": Failure of outward courage. "Loins": Re-
            sulting agony. "Faces": Ensuing death.
c. The prophet's exultation (2:11–13).
    1. Exultation expressed (verses 11, 12).
        (a) The question: "Where is the den of lions?"
        (b) Contrast of her passing with her former cruelty.
    2. Recognition of Jehovah.
        (a) His act of vengeance.
        (b) He was against Nineveh.
        (c) Therefore the overthrow is complete.

III. The vindication of vengeance (chapter 3).

Introductory Note. This last movement is devoted wholly to
the vindication of Jehovah in His action with regard to Nineveh,
and is a fitting defense of the introductory declarations concerning
His character. Vice and vengeance are shown in their inter-rela-
tion, the first as the reason of the second, and the second the in-
evitable result of the first.

a. Vice declared, and vengeance (3:1–3).
    1. Nineveh's vice (verse 1). "The bloody city."
        (a) Lies: State craft.
        (b) Rending: Administration.
        (c) Prey departeth not: Slavery.
    2. Vengeance (verses 2, 3).
        (a) Instrument: Graphic description; seven things men-
            tioned.
        (b) The slain.
b. Vice described, and vengeance (3:4–7).

1. Nineveh's vice (verse 4).
   (a) The national method: Whoredom; idolatrous prac-
       tices; witchcraft; all deceits.
   (b) The national influence: Selleth nations, and families.
2. Jehovah's vengeance (verses 5, 6). The exposure of vice.
3. Its unquestioned righteousness (verse 7). "Whence shall
   I seek comforters for thee?" The unanimous verdict of the
   nations is in harmony with the action of Jehovah.
c. Vice dissected, and vengeance (3:8–17).
   1. The vice (verses 8–10).
      (a) The question: "Art thou better?" The argument is
          that Thebes, though not so corrupt, was destroyed—
          her strength notwithstanding; how much more cer-
          tain is Nineveh's destruction, seeing her greater cor-
          ruption—her strength notwithstanding.
          (1) The strength of Thebes.
          (2) The destruction.
      (b) The deduction.
          (1) As to Thebes: Strength of no avail.
          (2) As to Nineveh: Corruption cancels strength.
   2. The vengeance (verses 11–17).
      (a) General statement (verse 11).
      (b) Particular description (verses 12–17).
          (1) The outer fortresses in the country, and the
              people there.
          (2) Gates of the land approaches to the capitol.
          (3) Then, the siege, and the fire.
          (4) The commercial center.
          (5) The governing center.
d. Vice destroyed (verses 18, 19).
   1. The end: Shepherds; nobles; people.
   2. The universal verdict: No healing; great rejoicing; because
      of universal oppression.

THE MESSAGE OF NAHUM

The message was to Judah, and if delivered in the period of the
Reformation under Manasseh it was singularly appropriate as a
message of encouragement and of solemn warning.

1.   Encouragement. Coming back from Bablyon it was probable that their hearts might be fearful lest their old enemy—Assyria—should trouble them again. Nahum ("the full of exceeding
comfort") speaking would greatly strengthen them (1:15).
Jehovah was still actively governing, and was on the side of those
returning to loyalty.

2.   Warning. Coming back from captivity in repentance for past
sins, a solemn warning is uttered against repentance which is
evanescent. Nineveh had repented, and had been spared; but having returned to her sins, the day of repentance is passed, and her
doom is determined. Jehovah is slow to anger, but He can by no
means clear the guilty.

C. The Permanent Message of Nahum

This picture of the doom of Nineveh must be studied in connection with the story of Jonah to discover its deepest lesson.

1. The first truth to be noted is that of the changelessness of
Jehovah. Some are inclined to think that this is a picture of the
changefulness of Jehovah. It is nothing of the kind. But did He
not spare Nineveh before when she repented, and does He not
say there is now no room for repentance, and that He has determined to destroy Nineveh? What appears to be change is due to
His changelessness. It is because God is unchanging in all the
eternal sublimities of His character that He changes in His dealings towards men.

A man said to me once concerning another man, "Why, he is
just as changeable as a weather vane on a steeple." What an un-
fortunate figure of speech! The most unchangeable thing there is
is a weather vane. But, you say, it is always changing; it is pointing
north, and south, and east, and west. Yes; but it is because of its
unchangeable principle that it shows from which way the wind is
coming. It is always unchangeable in its adhesion to principle. The
Almighty God is unchangeable. Today His word is the word of
tenderness, and tomorrow He smites. Has He changed? No,
Nineveh has changed. He has been the same throughout all His
dealings with men, and it is because He is unchangeable that
when a repentant nation repents of that repentance and goes back
to her sins, He repents again and smites her unto dust and sweeps

her away. The changelessness of Jehovah—that is the first message.

2. Another lesson is this solemn, terrible one, to be uttered almost with tears: there are limits to the forbearance of Jehovah. But where are they? Full opportunity is granted to every man and every nation, and God will never destroy a nation or a man until full opportunity has been granted. But the rejection of that full opportunity which expresses itself in direct defiance and challenge of God is the limit of God's patience. Never until a nation challenged God did God sweep a nation away as hopelessly as He swept away Nineveh. There lies the limit of His patience.

3. What else? This is a picture of the avenging God. The vengeance of God is actual, it is active, it is absolute. Yea, verily, verily, verily it is a fearful thing for willful, impenitent sinners to fall into the hands of the living God.

CHAPTER 8

HABAKKUK

1 The burden which Habakkuk the prophet did see.

2 O Lord, how long shall I cry, and thou wilt not hear! even cry out unto thee of violence, and thou wilt not save!

3 Why dost thou show me iniquity, and cause me to behold grievance? for spoiling and violence are before me: and there are that raise up strife and contention.

4 Therefore the law is slacked, and judgment doth never go forth: for the wicked doth compass about the righteous; therefore wrong judgment proceedeth.

5 Behold ye among the heathen, and regard, and wonder marvelously: for I will work a work in your days, which ye will not believe, though it be told you.

6 For, lo, I raise up the Chaldeans, that bitter and hasty nation, which shall march through the breadth of the land, to possess the dwelling places that are not theirs.

7 They are terrible and dreadful: their judgment and their dignity shall proceed of themselves.

8 Their horses also are swifter than the leopards, and are more fierce than the evening wolves: and their horsemen shall spread themselves, and their horsemen shall come from far;

they shall fly as the eagle that hasteth to eat.

9 They shall come all for violence: their faces shall sup up as the east wind, and they shall gather the captivity as the sand.

10 And they shall scoff at the kings, and the princes shall be a scorn unto them: they shall deride every stronghold; for they shall heap dust, and take it.

11 Then shall his mind change, and he shall pass over, and offend, imputing this his power unto his god.

12 Art thou not from everlasting, O Lord my God, mine Holy One? We shall not die. O Lord, thou hast ordained them for judgment; and, O mighty God, thou hast established them for correction.

13 Thou art of purer eyes than to behold evil, and canst not look on iniquity: wherefore lookest thou upon them that deal treacherously, and holdest thy tongue when the wicked devoureth the man that is more righteous than he?

14 And makest men as the fishes of the sea, as the creeping things, that have no ruler over them?

15 They take up all of them with the angle, they catch them in their net, and gather them in their drag: therefore they rejoice and are glad.

16 Therefore they sacrifice unto

their net, and burn incense unto their drag; because by them their portion is fat, and their meat plenteous.

17 Shall they therefore empty their net, and not spare continually to slay the nations?

CHAPTER 2

1 I will stand upon my watch, and set me upon the tower, and will watch to see what he will say unto me, and what I shall answer when I am reproved.

2 And the Lord answered me, and said, Write the vision, and make it plain upon tables, that he may run that readeth it.

3 For the vision is yet for an appointed time, but at the end it shall speak, and not lie: though it tarry, wait for it; because it will surely come, it will not tarry.

4 Behold, his soul which is lifted up is not upright in him: but the just shall live by his faith.

5 Yea also, because he transgresseth by wine, he is a proud man, neither keepeth at home, who enlargeth his desire as hell, and is as death, and cannot be satisfied, but gathereth unto him all nations, and heapeth unto him all people:

6 Shall not all these take up a parable against him, and a taunting proverb against him, and say, Woe to him that increaseth that which is not his! how long? and to him that ladeth himself with thick clay!

7 Shall they not rise up suddenly that shall bite thee, and awake that shall vex thee, and thou shalt be for booties unto them?

8 Because thou hast spoiled many nations, all the remnant of the people shall spoil thee; because of men's blood, and for the violence of the land, of the city, and all that dwell therein.

9 Woe to him that coveteth an evil covetousness to his house, that he may set his nest on high, that he may be delivered from the power of evil!

10 Thou hast consulted shame to thy house by cutting off many people, and hast sinned against thy soul.

11 For the stone shall cry out of the wall, and the beam out of the timber shall answer it.

12 Woe to him that buildeth a town with blood, and establisheth a city by iniquity!

13 Behold, is it not of the Lord of hosts that the people shall labor in the very fire, and the people shall weary themselves for very vanity?

14 For the earth shall be filled with the knowledge of the glory of the Lord, as the waters cover the sea.

15 Woe unto him that giveth his neighbor drink, that puttest thy bottle to him, and maketh him drunken also, that thou mayest look on their nakedness!

16 Thou art filled with shame for glory: drink thou also, and let thy foreskin be uncovered: the cup of the Lord's right hand shall be turned unto thee, and shameful spewing shall be on thy glory.

17 For the violence of Lebanon shall cover thee, and the spoil of beasts, which made them afraid, because of men's blood, and for the violence of the land, of the city, and of all that dwell therein.

18 What profiteth the graven image that the maker thereof hath graven it; the molten image, and a teacher of lies, that the maker of his work trusteth therein, to make dumb idols?

19 Woe unto him that saith to the wood, Awake; to the dumb stone, Arise, it shall teach! Behold, it is laid over with gold and silver, and there is no breath at all in the midst of it.

20 But the Lord is in his holy temple: let all the earth keep silence before him.

CHAPTER 3

1 A prayer of Habakkuk the prophet upon Shigionoth.

2 O Lord, I have heard thy speech, and was afraid: O Lord, revive thy work in the midst of the years, in the

midst of the years make known; in wrath remember mercy.

3 God came from Teman, and the Holy One from mount Paran. Selah. His glory covered the heavens, and the earth was full of his praise.

4 And his brightness was as the light; he had horns coming out of his hand: and there was the hiding of his power.

5 Before him went the pestilence, and burning coals went forth at his feet.

6 He stood, and measured the earth: he beheld, and drove asunder the nations; and the everlasting mountains were scattered, the perpetual hills did bow: his ways are everlasting.

7 I saw the tents of Cushan in affliction: and the curtains of the land of Midian did tremble.

8 Was the Lord displeased against the rivers? was thine anger against the rivers? was thy wrath against the sea, that thou didst ride upon thine horses and thy chariots of salvation?

9 Thy bow was made quite naked, according to the oaths of the tribes, even thy word. Selah. Thou didst cleave the earth with rivers.

10 The mountains saw thee, and they trembled: the overflowing of the water passed by: the deep uttered his voice, and lifted up his hands on high.

11 The sun and moon stood still in their habitation: at the light of thine arrows they went, and at the shining of thy glittering spear.

12 Thou didst march through the land in indignation, thou didst thresh the heathen anger.

13 Thou wentest forth for the salvation of thy people, even for salvation with thine anointed; thou woundedst the head out of the house of the wicked, by discovering the foundation unto the neck. Selah.

12 Thou didst strike through with his staves the head of his villages: they came out as a whirlwind to scatter me: their rejoicing was as to devour the poor secretly.

15 Thou didst walk through the sea with thine horses, through the heap of great waters.

16 When I heard, my belly trembled; my lips quivered at the voice: rottenness entered into my bones, and I trembled in myself, that I might rest in the day of trouble: when he cometh up unto the people, he will invade them with his troops.

17 Although the fig tree shall not blossom, neither shall fruit be in the vines; the labor of the olive shall fail, and the fields shall yield no meat; the flock shall be cut off from the fold, and there shall be no herd in the stalls:

18 Yet I will rejoice in the Lord, I will joy in the God of my salvation.

19 The Lord God is my strength, and he will make my feet like hinds' feet, and he will make me to walk upon mine high places. To the chief singer on my stringed instruments.

HABAKKUK—THE PROBLEMS OF FAITH

A. THE PROPHET AND HIS TIMES (Embraced)

I. *Dates.* Of Habakkuk nothing more is known than his name here declared. He was, perhaps, a Levite (see 3:19).

There is no very serious discrepancy in the opinions concerning the dates of his prophesying. Internal evidence brings it into relation with the Chaldean invasion, so that the range is 638–586 B.C. The Chaldean invasion was a punishment for Manasseh's sin, and yet did not come until after the death of Josiah, in the reign of Jehoiakim (II Kings 24:2, 3). When Habakkuk delivered his message the condition of things calling for reformation still existed (see 1:2–4). The probability is therefore that he prophesied during the closing years of Manasseh or during the reign of Amon or earlier than Zephaniah in the days of Josiah. If he prophesied later than Zephaniah he ignored the reform of Josiah. The attempts of modern critics to place the prophecy later is based upon the assumption that at the earlier date nothing was known of the Chaldean so exact as was the description of the prophet. This is practically to proceed on the hypothesis that prophecy as foretelling is impossible—an hypothesis which we do not accept.

II. *Characteristics.* A description of the times of Manasseh, Amon and the early days of Josiah—i.e., the four years from his accession at the age of eight, to the commencement of his reform at twelve (II Chronicles 34:3) is contained in II Kings 21 and 22. (Note especially: As to Manasseh, II Kings 21:9, 16; and as to Amon, II Kings 21:20.) The prophet's description in Habakkuk 1:2–4 would exactly fit this condition of things.

The book is a prophecy and yet its methods differ from any other. The burden of the prophet is that of the problems of permitted evil and the using of the Chaldeans as an instrument to scourge evildoers less wicked than they. Here we have a man of faith asking questions and receiving answers.

B. THE ANALYSIS OF THE PROPHECY

Introductory Note. A comparison of 1:2 with 3:19 gives us an indication of the true value of the book. Opening in mystery and questioning, it closes in certainty and affirmation. The contrast is startling. The first is almost a wail of despair, and the last is a shout of confidence. From the affirmation of faith's agnosticism we come to the confirmation of agnosticism's faith. The book is a movement from the one to the other. The door of exit and entrance is 2:4. The former part is the pathway leading to the door and the latter is the highway leading therefrom. Everything depends on seeing this central point.

I. *The prophet's problems* (1:1—2:4).

a. The first problem and answer (1:2–11).
   1. The problem (verses 2–4).
      (a) The apparent indifference of Jehovah to the prophet's prayer and to the condition of prevailing evil. The problem would never occur to a man who had not some faith. Take God away and there is no problem.
      (b) The condition described. "Violence": This word is the prophet's cry. It is as when one shouts, "Murder," and tells the condition. A condition of internal chaos. The law not administered.
   2. The answer (verses 5–11).
      (a) The divine affirmation and explanation of silence (verse 5). "I am working." "Ye will not believe."
      (b) The method described (verses 6–11). 2 *Kings* 24:2
         (1) The instrument named (verse 6).
         (2) The instrument described (verses 6–8).
         (3) The instrument acting (verses 9–10).
         (4) The final sin of the instrument (verse 11).
b. The second problem and answer 1:12—2:4).
   1. The problem (1:12–17). The prophet now begins by stating his faith.
      (a) Faith's affirmation (verse 12). *Deut* 32:4
      (b) Faith's acceptation of what God has said (verse 12).
      (c) Faith's astonishment (verses 13–17). The use of such an instrument is the new puzzle, for notwithstanding all Israel's sin they were more righteous than the Chaldeans. This constitutes the new problem.
   2. The prophet's attitude (2:1). This is the attitude of faith and honesty; he knows that God has an answer; he knows that God will give it; he will wait.
   3. The answer (2:2–4).
      (a) The command to write (verse 2).

    (1) Because it is not yet.

    (2) Plain for easy reading.

   (b) The certainty (verse 3).

    (1) An appointed time.

    (2) "Hasteth toward."

    (3) "Wait."

   (c) The vision (verse 4). This is a contrast between the "puffed up" and the righteous. The former is not upright and therefore is condemned. The latter acts on faith and therefore lives. The first is self-centered and is therefore doomed; the second is God-centered and therefore permanent.

Note. From here the prophecy is a proclamation of the contrast, and, therefore, an affirmation by faith of assurance in spite of appearances.

    II. The prophet's proclamations (2:5—3:19).

a. "Of the puffed up" (2:5–20).

 Note. In the proclamation concerning the "puffed up" the viewpoint is that of the sin of such, and the consequent judgments.

  1. Description of the "puffed up" (verse 5).

   (a) The first sentence and its difficulty. "Wine" not in the Greek or Syriac versions. Probably if used it was for the purpose of comparing the "puffed up" to one inflamed with wine.

   (b) The description: haughty; ambitious; conquering.

  2. Woes against the "puffed up." Mark the progress (verses 6–19).

   (a) Against ambition (verses 6–8).

    (1) Description.

    (2) Judgment: Revolt of oppressed and retribution in kind.

   (b) Against covetousness (verses 9–11).

    (1) Description: Lust for possession had led to destruction of many people.

    (2) Judgment: The subjugated break out against

the oppressor; the stones and beams of strong
houses testify.

(c) Against violence (verses 12–14).
   (1) Description: Cruel sufferings inflicted on the
      subjugated.
   (2) Judgment: The very cities so built shall be
      destroyed. So Jehovah will fill the earth with
      knowledge of Himself.
(d) Against insolence (verses 15–17).
   (1) Description: The brutal act of making a man
      drunk and then making sport of him.
   (2) Judgment: Retribution in the kind.
(e) Against idolatry (verses 18, 19).
   (1) Description: Wholly satirical.
   (2) Judgment: The unanswering gods.

3. Final statement of the prophet (verse 20). This declares
that the prophet has found a solution, and it is well for all
the earth to keep silence before Jehovah. The apparent
strength of wickedness is false; Jehovah reigns.

b. Of the righteous (chapter 3).

Note. In the proclamation concerning the righteous the viewpoint is that of the majesty of Jehovah, and the consequent triumph
of His people.

1. The initial prayer (verse 2).
(a) The declaration: "I have heard the report and am
afraid." At the beginning he cried out for divine
interference. Now that he sees it approaching, he
pleads that mercy may be remembered.
(b) The prayer: He is afraid, yet he prays that God will
revive His work (cf. 1:5).

2. The God in whom faith is centered (verses 3–15).

Note. There are very diversified opinions concerning the actual
historical references in this section. I have been utterly unable to
find anything approaching consecutiveness or clearness. Indeed
it seems to be a mixture of incidental allusions in a general description of the glory and power of God. Yet it may be that there is a
systematized allusion to all the ways of God with His people. The
final subject of the prophecy is that "the just shall live by faith,"

and it may be well that the illustrations are from the history of the
people embodying that principle in history and in life.

    (a) The first movement (verses 3–7).

        (1) "God came": Abraham; Temen; Paran.

        (2) Poetic description.

        (3) Cushan and Midian; Asiatic and Nomadic tribes.

    (b) The exodus (verses 8–10). Moses.

        (1) The rhetorical question.

        (2) The description.

    (c) The possession (verses 11–15). Joshua. The possession described.

  3. The fear and the faith of the just. "I heard" (verses 16–19).

    (a) The fear (the difficulty of latter part).

    (b) The faith. The contemplation of the judgment of the "puffed up" fills him with fear, yet he triumphs in God.

        (1) Desolation described.

        (2) The determination to rejoice.

        (3) The reason declared.

THE MESSAGE OF HABAKKUK

Does not the message of the prophet lie all along the pages?
Notice only this: the prophet's frank admission at the beginning
of the problems which confront faith; then, through the process
of the prophet's dealing with God, we have a declaration, clear
and unmistakable, of the present activity of Jehovah. This issues
in an affirmation of confidence, than which there is nothing finer
in the whole of the Old Testament. Here was a man living by his
faith and declaring a message out of his own life by faith concerning the permanence of life by faith. His message was surely to the
remnant of Israel, and was for the encouragement of their faith.
It was a message concerning the self-consuming nature of self-
centered life. Let your mind go back over it, and see how true it is,
and then trace it all down the ages: the self-consuming nature of
self-centered life. Jesus, what wondrous things He said. "He that
saveth his life shall lose it"; not, shall lose another life by and by,

but his present life. The man that tries to conserve himself and
lives for himself loses himself. On the other hand, we have a revelation of the absolute triumph over circumstances and over all
enemies, of the God-centered life. "He that loseth his life shall
find"—life beyond? No, no—he shall find his life. This is a thing
you cannot explain exactly, and yet it can be demonstrated by the
experience of all men in all ages. Do not take too wide an outlook
for the present; take a narrow one: yourself. Am I living a self-
centered life? Then I am losing my life for which I live. I am not
getting out of it what God put in it. I do not know what living is
if I am living a self-centered life. Clouds are always round about
me; darkness is over all my path. Self-centered life consumes itself.

Am I living a God-centered life? Then I am finding it. What?
My own life. Every power of my being is akin to divinity, and when
all the powers of my being are lived with respect to God, they are
being glorified and ennobled. Oh, that this gospel could be
preached and understood! "The just lives by faith."

C. The Permanent Message

I. *Stated.* The permanent message of this prophecy is, first, of
the governing God. He acts in wisdom and in righteousness, notwithstanding all appearances to the contrary. Before emphasizing
this, let me go a step further. Men of faith are always the men that
have to confront problems. Blot God out, and your problems are
all ended. If there is no God in heaven, then we have no problem
about sin and suffering; no problem about the slum and the tene-
ment house and the oppression of the poor and all the prosperity
of the rich and sinful. But the moment you admit the existence
of an all-powerful governing God, you are face to face with your
problems. If you say that you have none, I question the strength of
your faith. And yet, oh, these paradoxes, these contradictions of
spiritual life! It is the man of faith who, having the problem, always
finds its solution, not always in an immediate explanation of the
problem confronted, but in the new confidence that God can make
no mistake. If there is one verse more wonderful, more precious
along this line than any other in all the inspired revelation, it is

this that comes to the mind of the trusting soul whenever a problem confronts us, "Shall not the judge of all the earth do right?" That is the only place of rest. Knowledge of God creates problems; fuller knowledge of God answers them every one. That seems to me to be the great lesson.

Then we learn that, notwithstanding all appearance to the contrary, God is working and whatever His method may be, we must learn to pray that He will work on while in faith we sing the song of deliverance. Thus the one central lesson is that "The just shall live by faith"; the "puffed-up" shall perish, and the faithful are sure to triumph both in sorrow and through sorrow.

II. *Applied.* Today there are two principles of life in the world and only two. The principle of the "puffed-up," who are self-centered and conditioned by circumstance; and the principle of the righteous by faith, who are God-centered and God-circumferenced. Centered in God and circumferenced of God? Yes, for He is the sphere in which you live and move and have your being. That is the truth about the life of faith. When a man has his faith in God, God is at the center of his being and is at the circumference of his being; He is everywhere. Men who are self-centered and circumstance-conditioned may seem to succeed, and the men who are God-centered and God-circumstanced often seem to be in extremis. How often for the saints the fig tree has not blossomed, and there has been no herd in the stall! How often the wicked has been seen spreading himself like a green bay tree! But this book teaches us that the true viewpoint is that obtained when the discussion of these problems is carried into the presence of God, giving to Him the opportunity to tell us His secrets; then we shall find that in the green bay tree is the worm that dieth not which is already sapping away its life, and also that in the barrenness of today's outlook for the people of God are the fertilizing forces that will bring a harvest for tomorrow. You cannot be a man of faith and live in a day. You do not live in a day if you are a man of faith. When Habakkuk tried living in a day, he wailed, "O God, you are doing nothing!" but when he began to breathe the subconsciousness of eternity and touched the infinitude of deity, then he said: "God is doing everything, and if I have any one fear it is lest his wrath which is to overwhelm it too terrible. O Lord, remember mercy." The problems of faith must be submitted to God for His answer; and whenever a soul does that, there will come such revelations as shall create a song of triumph even while the heart abides in the presence of a present sadness.

CHAPTER 9

ZEPHANIAH

CHAPTER 1

1 The word of the Lord which came unto Zephaniah the son of Cushi, the son of Gedaliah, the son of Amariah, the son of Hizkiah, in the days of Josiah the son of Amon, king of Judah.

2 I will utterly consume all things from off the land, saith the Lord.

3 I will consume man and beast; I will consume the fowls of the heaven, and the fishes of the sea, and the stumblingblocks with the wicked; and I will cut off man from off the land, saith the Lord.

4 I will also stretch out mine hand upon Judah, and upon all the inhabitants of Jerusalem; and I will cut off the remnant of Baal from this place, and the name of the Chemarim with the priests;

5 And them that worship the host of heaven upon the housetops; and them that worship and that swear by the Lord, and that swear by Malcham;

6 And them that are turned back from the Lord; and those that have not sought the Lord, nor inquired for him.

7 Hold thy peace at the presence of the Lord God: for the day of the Lord is at hand: for the Lord hath prepared a sacrifice, he hath bid his guests.

8 And it shall come to pass in the day of the Lord's sacrifice, that I will punish the princes, and the king's children, and all such as are clothed with strange apparel.

9 In the same day also will I punish all those that leap on the threshold, which fill their masters' houses with violence and deceit.

10 And it shall come to pass in that day, saith the Lord, that there shall be the noise of a cry from the fish gate, and a howling from the second, and a great crashing from the hills.

11 Howl, ye inhabitants of Maktesh, for all the merchant people are cut down; all they that bear silver are cut off.

12 And it shall come to pass at that time, that I will search Jerusalem with candles, and punish the men that are settled on their lees: that say in their heart, The Lord will not do good, neither will he do evil.

13 Therefore, their goods shall become a booty, and their houses a desolation: they shall also build houses, but not inhabit them; and they shall plant vineyards, but not drink the wine thereof.

14 The great day of the Lord is near, it is near, and hasteth greatly, even the voice of the day of the Lord: the mighty man shall cry there bitterly.

15 That day is a day of wrath, a day of trouble and distress, a day of wasteness and desolation, a day of darkness and gloominess, a day of clouds and thick darkness,

16 A day of the trumpet and alarm against the fenced cities, and against the high towers.

17 And I will bring distress upon men, that they shall walk like blind men, because they have sinned against the Lord: and their blood shall be poured out as dust, and their flesh as the dung.

18 Neither their silver nor their gold shall be able to deliver them in the day of the Lord's wrath; but the whole land shall be devoured by the fire of his jealousy: for he shall make even a speedy riddance of all them that dwell in the land.

CHAPTER 2

1 Gather yourselves together, yea, gather together, O nation not desired;

2 Before the decree bring forth, before the day pass as the chaff, before the fierce anger of the Lord come upon you, before the day of the Lord's anger come upon you.

3 Seek ye the Lord, all ye meek of the earth, which have wrought his judgment; seek righteousness, seek meekness: it may be ye shall be hid in the day of the Lord's anger.

4 For Gaza shall be forsaken, and Ashkelon a desolation: they shall drive out Ashdod at the noonday, and Ekron shall be rooted up.

5 Woe unto the inhabitants of the seacoast, the nation of the Cherethites! the word of the Lord is against you; O Canaan, the land of the Philistines, I will even destroy thee, that there shall be no inhabitant.

6 And the seacoast shall be dwellings and cottages for shepherds, and folds for flocks.

7 And the coast shall be for the remnant of the house of Judah; they shall feed thereupon: in the houses of Ashkelon shall they lie down in the evening: for the Lord their God shall visit them, and turn away their captivity.

8 I have heard the reproach of Moab, and the revilings of the children of Ammon, whereby they have reproached my people, and magnified themselves against their border.

9 Therefore, as I live, saith the Lord of hosts, the God of Israel, Surely Moab shall be as Sodom, and the children of Ammon as Gomorrah, even the breeding of nettles, and salt-pits, and a perpetual desolation: the residue of my people shall spoil them, and the remnant of my people shall possess them.

10 This shall they have for their pride, because they have reproached and magnified themselves against the people of the Lord of hosts.

11 The Lord will be terrible unto them: for he will famish all the gods of the earth; and men shall worship him, every one from his place, even all the isles of the heathen.

12 Ye Ethiopians also, ye shall be slain by my sword.

13 And he will stretch out his hand against the north, and destroy Assyria; and will make Nineveh a desolation, and dry like a wilderness.

14 And flocks shall lie down in the midst of her, all the beasts of the nations: both the cormorant and the bittern shall lodge in the upper lintels of it; their voice shall sing in the windows; desolation shall be in the thresholds: for he shall uncover the cedar work.

15 This is the rejoicing city that dwelt carelessly, that said in her heart, I am, and there is none besides me: how is she become a desolation, a place for beasts to lie down in!

every one that passeth by her shall hiss, and wag his hand.

CHAPTER 3

1 Woe to her that is filthy and polluted, to the oppressing city!

2 She obeyed not the voice; she received not correction; she trusted not in the Lord; she drew not near to her God.

3 Her princes within her are roaring lions; her judges are evening wolves; they gnaw not the bones till the morrow.

4 Her prophets are light and treacherous persons: her priests have polluted the sanctuary, they have done violence to the law.

5 The just Lord is in the midst thereof; he will not do iniquity; every morning doth he bring his judgment to light, he faileth not; but the unjust knoweth no shame.

6 I have cut off the nations: their towers are desolate; I made their streets waste, that none passeth by: their cities are destroyed, so that there is no man, that there is none inhabitant.

7 I said, Surely, thou wilt fear me, thou wilt receive instruction; so their dwelling should not be cut off, howsoever I punished them: but they rose early, and corrupted all their doings.

8 Therefore wait ye upon me, saith the Lord, until the day that I rise up to the prey: for my determination is to gather the nations, that I may assemble the kingdoms, to pour upon them mine indignation, even all my fierce anger: for all the earth shall be devoured with the fire of my jealousy.

9 For then will I turn to the people a pure language, that they may all call upon the name of the Lord, to serve him with one consent.

10 From beyond the rivers of Ethiopia my suppliants, even the daughter of my dispersed, shall bring mine offering.

11 In that day shalt thou not be ashamed for all thy doings, wherein thou hast transgressed against me: for then I will take away out of the midst of thee them that rejoice in thy pride, and thou shalt no more be haughty because of my holy mountain.

12 I will also leave in the midst of thee an afflicted and poor people, and they shall trust in the name of the Lord.

13 The remnant of Israel shall not do iniquity, nor speak lies; neither shall a deceitful tongue be found in their mouth: for they shall feed and lie down, and none shall make them afraid.

14 Sing, O daughter of Zion; shout, O Israel; be glad and rejoice with all the heart, O daughter of Jerusalem.

15 The Lord hath taken away thy judgments, he hath cast out thine enemy: the King of Israel, even the Lord, is in the midst of thee: thou shalt not see evil any more.

16 In that day it shall be said to Jerusalem, Fear thou not: and to Zion, Let not thine hands be slack.

17 The Lord thy God in the midst of thee is mighty; he will save, he will rejoice over thee with joy; he will rest in his love, he will joy over thee with singing.

18 I will gather them that are sorrowful for the solemn assembly, who are of thee, to whom the reproach of it was a burden.

19 Behold, at that time I will undo all that afflict thee: and I will save her that halteth, and gather her that was driven out; and I will get them praise and fame in every land where they have been put to shame.

20 At that time will I bring you again, even in the time that I gather you: for I will make you a name and a praise among all people of the earth, when I turn back your captivity before your eyes, saith the Lord.

ZEPHANIAH—THE SEVERITY AND GOODNESS OF GOD

A. The Prophet and His Times

I. *Dates.* This prophecy is clearly dated as having come to Zephaniah in the reign of Josiah. He reigned thirty-one years, 638–608 B.C. During what period of his reign did Zephaniah prophesy? That is the general difficulty.

Josiah began to reign when he was eight years old.

In 630 he began to seek God; sixteen years old (eighth year of reign).

In 626 he began to purge Jerusalem; twenty years old (twelfth year of reign).

In 620 he began to repair the temple, found the Book and celebrated the Passover; twenty-six years old (eighteenth year of reign).

In 608 he died; thirty-eight years old (thirtieth year of reign).

If, as is most probable, Zephaniah was descended from King Hezekiah, he was the fourth generation from Hezekiah, while Josiah was third in direct descent from Hezekiah. Hezekiah in all probability then would be no older than Josiah; perhaps younger. Therefore his prophesying would necessarily have come not later than the reformation period.

Hezekiah began to reign when he was twenty-five years old and reigned twenty-nine years (II Chronicles 29:1).

Manasseh began to reign when he was twelve years old and reigned fifty-five years (II Chronicles 33:21).

Amon began to reign when he was twenty-two years old and reigned two years (II Chronicles 33:21).

Josiah began to reign when he was eight years old.

Manasseh, therefore was forty-five years old when Amon was born and Amon was sixteen years old when Josiah was born. There was thus sixty-one years between the birth of Manasseh and Josiah. In Zechariah's genealogy, this period was covered by the generations of Hezekiah, Amariah, Gedaliah, Cushi, and Zephaniah. The prophet must therefore have been a young man when the word of the Lord came unto him, perhaps during Josiah's reformation or about 626–630 B.C.

II. *Characteristics.* It is a remarkable thing that Zephaniah ignores the reformation. None of the prophets were more scathing in their denunciation referring to Huldah's prophecy at the finding of the law (II Chronicles 34:22–28; see also Jeremiah).

Zephaniah's severity in dealing with court life is also explained by his intimate acquaintance with it as a prince. The reformation was due to Josiah, and was as thorough as he could make it, but so far as the people were concerned it was worthless, being only conformity to the command of the king. It had not its root in true godliness in the nation as a whole. Zephaniah therefore ignores the whole movement and speaks as to a people utterly corrupt.

B. The Analysis of the Prophecy

I. The day of wrath with an appeal (1:2—2:15).

a. The day of wrath (1:2–18).
   1. Announced in general terms (verses 2–6).
      (a) Comprehensive statement (verse 2). "I will consume all."
      (b) The destruction of the creation as far as it is evil (verse 3).
         (1) Man and the sphere of his dominion.
         (2) The stumbling block.
         (3) The race.
      (c) The local application (verses 4–6).
         (1) Judah and Jerusalem.
         (2) Remnant of Baal, name of Chemarim with the priests. This may be an allusion to the Reformation.
         (3) The worshipers. Note the classes: open idolatry; mixed worship; backsliding; never converted.
   2. Described particularly (verses 7–13).
      (a) Summons (verse 7). "Hush!" Here we have the presence of Jehovah; the day of Jehovah and the sacrifice of Jehovah, all referring to judgment.
      (b) The procedures (verses 8–13).
         (1) The princes; the king's sons, "clothed with foreign apparel."
         (2) The extortioners—filling government offices.

        (3) The city: fish gate; second quarter; the hills.

        (4) The merchant men caught in a mortar.

        (5) The men settled on their less, i.e., living on their wealth in idleness and indifference.

   3. Described as to character (verses 14–18).

      (a) The nearness of the day (verse 14).

      (b) The day (verses 15, 16). Graphic description.

      (c) The activity of Jehovah in that day (verses 17, 18). The terrible judgment on sin: "An end—a terrible end!"

b. The appeal (chapter 2).

   1. The cry to the nations (verses 1, 2).

      (a) "Pull yourselves together."

      (b) The day of opportunity passes.

   2. The call to the remnant.

      (a) There is a remnant.

      (b) These are urged to renewed devotion.

   3. The argument with which he enforces his appeal (verses 4–15).

      (a) Judgment.

        (1) Nations on the west, Philistia (verses 4–7).

        (2) Nations on the west, Moab and Amon (verses 8–11).

        (3) Nations on the west, Ethiopia (verse 12).

        (4) Nations on the north, Assyria (verses 13–15).

      (b) Declarations concerning remnant: They are to inhabit the land from which the enemy is to be turned out.

        (1) On the west (verses 6, 7).

        (2) On the east (verse 9). Notice that the references to the remnant are confined to the west and east.

II. *The day of wrath and its issue* (*chapter* 3).

a. The day of wrath (3:1–8).

   1. The woe declared (verse 1). The prophet now returns to speak of Jerusalem, the supremely guilty city.

   2. The reason declared (verses 2–7).

      (a) The city as a whole (verse 2). "Obey not. . .

Receive not corrections. . . . Trusted not on Jehovah. . . . Drew not near her God."

(b) Her rulers who are responsible for the condition
(verses 3, 4). Princes, judges, prophets and priests.

(c) Jehovah (verses 5–7). His presence unheeded. His
deliverances responded to with increased corruption.

3. The final word (verse 8).

(a) "Wait for me." This is the first gleam of hope. The
very hopelessness of the sin of the people makes
divine action necessary. In that is hope.

(b) Judgment must come, but it is a prelude.

b. The issue of the day (3:9–20).

Note. From this point on the prophecy is Messianic. Zephaniah
gives no picture of the Suffering Servant, nor any hint of the
method. He only deals with the ultimate result to Israel. The
judgments have yet to come in the calendar of human history, but
in the purpose of God their removal is decreed.

1. The gathering of a remnant (verses 9–13).

(a) The peoples (verse 9).

(b) My supplicants (verses 10–13).

2. The remnant addressed (verses 14–20).

(a) Singing and gladness (verses 14, 15).

(1) Enjoined (verse 14).

(2) The reasons (verse 15). The cast out foes. The
resident King.

(b) Courage and service (verses 16, 17).

(1) Enjoined (verse 16).

(2) The reasons (verse 17). The resident King.
Mighty to save. Full of the tenderness of His
love. Resting, rejoicing, singing. Here we see
the Motherhood of God. "He has a father's arm
but a mother's heart."

(c) The reversal of all the sorrow (verses 18–20).

THE MESSAGE OF ZEPHANIAH

Perhaps no prophet gave a more definite declaration of the terrors of the divine judgment against sin than did Zephaniah, and

this is emphasized by his ignoring utterly the reforms which he saw and knew to be insincere on the part of the people.

There can be little doubt, I think, that Zephaniah was of the royal house, and of about the same age as Josiah, if not a little younger. Probably, therefore, he uttered his prophecy at about the age of twenty-four or twenty-five, or just when the reformation under Josiah was in progress; and yet the remarkable thing is that Zephaniah makes no reference to the reformation. He speaks only of the sin of the people and the swift judgment of God that is coming upon the sin. That is to be accounted for, I think, by referring to the story of the finding of the book of the Law by Hilkiah, and to the fact that Josiah then sent to the prophetess Huldah. She answered the message delivered by declaring that because Josiah was sincere God would spare him and he should not share in or see the judgments that were to come. But she declared emphatically that the curses they found written in the book of the Law were certain to come upon the people. Put these two things together and I think we have the key, the revelation, of the true condition of affairs. The reforms initiated by Josiah were joined in by the people simply because the king led, and not out of any real heart repentance. That is borne out by the history of the times that followed. The reforms were not lasting, and consequently Zephaniah, speaking under the inspiration of the Spirit and perfectly understanding that the outward appearance of reform was not indicative of a true change of heart toward God, took no notice of the reform; he dealt only with the sin and with the corruption. He therefore more definitely perhaps than any other prophet declared the terrors of the divine judgment against sin, and the larger part of his message is given to the announcement of the judgment of God upon the sin of His own people.

And yet to Zephaniah has fallen the lot of uttering the very sweetest love song of the Old testament. That exquisite picture of the motherhood of God which we have in the third chapter in which he gives us a picture of God rejoicing over His people, silent in His love, and suddenly breaking in upon the silence of His love with a song of delight. What revelation of the heart of God is more exquisite than this: the picture of God singing for very joy over His people! It is a picture of the motherhood of God.

One line of modern criticism has declined to receive this latter

section of the third chapter as Zephaniah's prophecy because
of its tenderness. We are told that the man who wrote things so
scathing, scorching, severe as we find in the first part could not
be the man who wrote the tender, exquisite love music of the
latter part. I think that I need not argue that any further than
to say to you that no man is ever capable of giving utterance to
the truth of the deepest love of God save he who is so conscious
of the light of God that he can speak of His judgments in tones
terrific. There are two essential words about God in our Bible:
"God is love," and "God is light." These are complementary the
one to the other. The man who lives in the light knows the love,
and the man who lives in the love walks in the light; and the
man who, living in the light and the love, speaks of the light
as it searches and reveals sin and who denounces it, is the man
who out of the love can sing the song of the victory of love
over sin as the sinner is redeemed. It is not without significance
that the man whom Jesus spoke of in connection with his brother
as Boanerges, "the son of thunder," is known as a son of conso-
lation and the apostle of love. It is also significant that in the
writings of that same man, John, the words that recur all the
way through are such words as "commandments, commandments,
commandments," and "love, love, love." Zephaniah lived so near
to the light that he knew the love, and lived so absolutely in the
love that he walked in the light. Because of that intimate acquaintance with God he said these scorching, scathing, searing
things against sin, and then suddenly the message merged into
the sweet, tender love song in which he unveiled, as no other Old
Testament writer has, the very heart of God, moved with the
love of motherhood, singing over the child after the silence of
that love has been broken.

What then is the message that Zephaniah delivered to his own
day? It is a message of the unity of the divine method. We see
God's absolute refusal to excuse sin because of His love, and we
see His love acting in consuming wrath in order to secure the
final realization of its most tender purpose. If you cut out that
last part of Zephaniah, then he has no distinctive message. It is
not the first part, but the second part, of the prophecy that is
the message of Zephaniah. It is that peculiar union formed by
the denunciation of sin that is so severe, and the annunciation

of love that is so tender. These two together give us the great message that Zephaniah delivered to his people: love cannot excuse sin, but love will at last find a way to realize its purpose in spite of all the sin of the people.[*]

How this great lesson was needed by Israel! The lesson of the love of God expressing itself in anger against sin, and the lesson that the very judgment of sin was the proof of His love and the measure by which He worked toward the final accomplishment of His love. Israel utterly failed to learn the message of Zephaniah. She has not learned it yet, but she will learn it, and the day will come when all these prophecies shall be fulfilled, must be fulfilled, in the history of God's ancient people.

C. THE PERMANENT MESSAGES FROM THIS PROPHECY

What is the message for us as well as for Israel? What are the great truths that we may take hold of and apply to our own day and generation? What are the things here that our own souls must learn, and that are to abide with us in our living, and in our work? The notes that come to me out of the prophecy are these: (1) Love's passionate anger; (2) love's patient purpose; and (3) love's ultimate victory. You may think that this is always the same message: Love. Exactly so. That is the supreme revelation of the minor prophets to my soul. The only message I find whenever I come to the close of one of these prophecies is something about God's love. When I decided to take up these minor prophets, I expected to study a very magnificent section of prophecy in which I should hear stern, hard, magnificent Hebrew prophets thunder-

---

[*] Do not take anything I say in connection with this prophecy concerning Israel and stretch it out of its proportion and make it apply to other questions than that under discussion. When I said something like this in our study of Hosea last year, I had a most eloquent and lengthy epistle showing me that the logical sequence of my teaching was the final restoration of all men. You have no right to make any such logical sequence from anything here. That subject is not under consideration. This refers to God's earthly people, Israel. If you are going to make deductions concerning all men from this revelation concerning Israel as a nation, do not forget that they who fell in the wilderness did not enter into God's rest, and there were those who in spite of covenant blessing nevertheless missed the realization, and there will be all the way through. Love will have its triumph, not necessarily in the case of every individual, but in the fulfilling of the great purpose of God concerning His people.

ing against sin. I found this even more than I had expected, but
the supreme thing in every one of their prophecies is that the
God with whom these men were intimate was known by them
to be a God of tender love, of infinite compassion, angry because
He loves, dealing in wrath upon the basis of His love, and proceeding through judgment to the ultimate purpose of His heart.
It is the heartbeat of God that throbs through these passages.

1. Zephaniah terrifies me as I begin to read him. As I read
those searching, awful things which he says, and see the way in
which he tears the veil from the sin of the people and leaves sin
in all its naked, awful horror, and then pronounces upon it the
swift, fearful doom of God's vengeance, I am startled and afraid.
But I read on, and presently I hear this little word, which is
the first note from the trumpet of redemption, "Wait for me, saith
Jehovah." From thenceforward all the message merges into this
endless music of a psalm of love, and I learn that the passionate
anger of the first chapters is but the anger of love. Yes, God is
angry with the sinner every day; but why? Because the sinner
is ruining himself. God never comes to a man in anger to burn
up, or destroy, or strike, save in order that He may save and
bless. All God's anger is the expression of His love.

2. Then I find in this book the patient purpose of God, the
patient purpose of love, and again I go back to that little word
that is to me the arresting word. When the last fearful thing is
said about the judgment, then comes the word, "Yet wait for
me." Oh, the patience of love as it gave to a man who had so
dire and dreadful a message of judgment to declare, the sweet
anthem of the love of the heart of God. The experience which
a man or a people has of God's love depends upon their attitude
toward it. That is the great deduction from these great truths.
Are you impure? God's love will destroy you. Are you repentant
and turning your face toward Him? God's love will restore you.
Everything depends on your attitude toward Him. If you are impure, God's love will destroy you, because His love is so great
it cannot be confined to you, it takes in your neighbor. There
have been times when God has had to sweep out a nation for
the sake of the nations lying about. There have been times when
God has had to take a father out of his family to give his children
a chance to be pure. Why did God destroy the nationality of

Israel for centuries? Because of the nations lying round about. It was not vindictiveness, but it was because Jerusalem and Israel had received the light and they had hidden it, and the surrounding nations were still in darkness. Then Jerusalem must be swept out and the people destroyed for a period in order that the nations around might be reached through another instrumentality. And notwithstanding all I read in prophecy, I believe that if Christendom fail to bear its clean, clear testimony to God among the nations, He will cast out these nations. Does that upset all your theories about what is going to happen? So did the casting out of Israel upset all Israel's theories about what was going to happen. Who are we to say that God may not make some other interpolation while He rejects His own Church for a period in order that He may do His great work? I do not say that He will, but we must learn this great principle: that His love is so great that the impure must be destroyed for the sake of the larger issues and the larger values.

3. But thank God, wherever there is a repentant heart, even in the midst of utter corruption, He takes that one, He brings it to Himself, and breaks into song over the restoration of a soul.

CHAPTER 10

HAGGAI

CHAPTER 1

1 In the second year of Darius the king, in the sixth month, in the first day of the month, came the word of the Lord by Haggai the prophet unto Zerubbabel the son of Shealtiel, governor of Judah, and to Joshua the son of Josedech, the high priest, saying,

2 Thus speaketh the Lord of hosts, saying, This people say, The time is not come, the time that the Lord's house should be built.

3 Then came the word of the Lord by Haggai the prophet, saying,

4 Is it time for you, O ye, to dwell in your ceiled houses, and this house lie waste?

5 Now therefore thus saith the Lord of hosts; Consider your ways.

6 Ye have sown much, and bring in little; ye eat, but ye have not enough; ye drink, but ye are not filled with drink; ye clothe you, but there is none warm; and he that earneth wages, earneth wages to put it into a bag with holes.

7 Thus saith the Lord of hosts; Consider your ways.

8 Go up to the mountain, and bring wood, and build the house; and I will take pleasure in it, and I will be glorified, saith the Lord.

9 Ye looked for much, and, lo, it came to little; and when ye brought it home, I did blow upon it. Why? saith the Lord of hosts. Because of mine house that is waste, and ye run every man unto his own house.

10 Therefore the heaven over you is stayed from dew, and the earth is stayed from her fruit.

11 And I called for a drought upon the land, and upon the mountains, and upon the corn, and upon the new wine, and upon the oil, and upon that which the ground bringeth forth, and upon men, and upon cattle, and upon all the labor of the hands.

12 Then Zerubbabel the son of Shealtiel, and Joshua the son of Josedech, the high priest, with all the remnant of the people, obeyed the voice of the Lord their God, and the words of Haggai the prophet, as the Lord their God had sent him, and the people did fear before the Lord.

13 Then spake Haggai the Lord's messenger in the Lord's message unto the people, saying, I am with you, saith the Lord.

14 And the Lord stirred up the spirit of Zerubbabel the son of Shealtiel, governor of Judah, and the spirit of Joshua the son of Josedech, the high priest, and the spirit of all the remnant of the people; and they came and did work in the house of the Lord of hosts, their God.

15 In the four and twentieth day of the sixth month, in the second year of Darius the king.

CHAPTER 2

1 In the seventh month, in the one and twentieth day of the month, came the word of the Lord by the prophet Haggai, saying,

2 Speak now to Zerubbabel the son of Shealtiel, governor of Judah, and to Joshua the son of Josedech, the high priest, and to the residue of the people, saying,

3 Who is left among you that saw this house in her first glory? and how do ye see it now? is it not in your eyes in comparison of it as nothing?

4 Yet now be strong, O Zerubbabel, saith the Lord; and be strong, O Joshua, son of Josedech, the high priest; and be strong, all ye people of the land, saith the Lord, and work: for I am with you, saith the Lord of hosts:

5 According to the word that I covenanted with you when ye came out of Egypt, so my Spirit remaineth among you: fear ye not.

6 For thus saith the Lord of hosts; Yet once, it is a little while, and I will shake the heavens, and the earth, and the sea, and the dry land;

7 And I will shake all nations, and the Desire of all nations shall come: and I will fill this house with glory, saith the Lord of hosts.

8 The silver is mine, and the gold is mine, saith the Lord of hosts.

9 The glory of this latter house shall be greater than of the former, saith the Lord of hosts: and in this place will I give peace, saith the Lord of hosts.

10 In the four and twentieth day of the ninth month, in the second year of Darius, came the word of the Lord by Haggai the prophet, saying,

11 Thus saith the Lord of hosts; Ask now the priests concerning the law, saying,

12 If one bear holy flesh in the skirt of his garment, and with his skirt do touch bread, or pottage, or wine, or oil, or any meat, shall it be holy? And the priests answered and said, No.

13 Then said Haggai, If one that is unclean by a dead body touch any of these, shall it be unclean? And the priests answered and said, It shall be unclean.

14 Then answered Haggai, and said, So is this people, and so is this nation before me, saith the Lord; and so is every work of their hands; and that which they offer there is unclean.

15 And now, I pray you, consider from this day and upward, from before a stone was laid upon a stone in the temple of the Lord:

16 Since those days were, when one came to a heap of twenty measures, there were but ten: when one came to the pressvat for to draw out fifty vessels out of the press, there were but twenty.

17 I smote you with blasting and with mildew and with hail in all the labors of your hands; yet ye turned not to me, saith the Lord.

18 Consider now from this day and upward, from the four and twentieth day of the ninth month, even from the day that the foundation of the Lord's temple was laid, consider it.

19 Is the seed yet in the barn? yea, as yet the vine, and the fig tree, and the pomegranate, and the olive tree, hath not brought forth: from this day will I bless you.

20 And again the word of the Lord came unto Haggai in the four and twentieth day of the month, saying,

21 Speak to Zerubbabel, governor of Judah, saying, I will shake the heavens and the earth;

22 And I will overthrow the throne of kingdoms, and I will destroy the strength of the kingdoms of the heathen; and I will overthrow the chariots, and those that ride in them; and

the horses and their riders shall come down, every one by the sword of his brother.

23 In that day, saith the Lord of hosts, will I take thee, O Zerubbabel,

my servant, the son of Shealtiel, saith the Lord, and will make thee as a signet: for I have chosen thee, saith the Lord of hosts.

POST EXILE

HAGGAI—THE DUTY OF COURAGE

ZECH
MALACHI   *520 BC*

A. The Prophet and His Times

I. *Dates.* Of Haggai's personal history nothing is known, but the dating of our prophecy is very exact. It is noticeable that for the first time a Gentile date is given and Israel counts its days by the reign of an outside king. Darius reigned from 521 B.C. to 486 B.C., so that Haggai's four messages fell within about four months in the years 520–519 B.C. He and Zechariah were contemporary and in part their prophesying alternated as follows:

Second year of Darius, 6th month, 1st day, Haggai's 1st message.

Second year of Darius, 7th month, 21st day, Haggai's 2nd message.

Second year of Darius, 8th month, Zechariah's 1st message.

Second year of Darius, 9th month, 24th day, Haggai's 3rd message.

Second year of Darius, 9th month, 24th day, Haggai's 4th message.

Second year of Darius, 11th month, 24th day, Zechariah's 2nd message.

Fourth year of Darius, 9th month, 4th day, Zechariah's 3rd message.

II. *Charatceristics.* For the understanding of these conditions which existed in Haggai's day, we have to go back a little in the history of Israel. Let this be done by the tabulation of events. *50,000 Jews?* 536 B.C. Return from Babylon under Zerubbabel (Ezra 3:1–4). 1—Altar built. 2—Sacrifices offered. 3—Feast of Tabernacles. 535 B.C. Foundations of the temple laid. Opposition of Samaritans and the building stopped. *14 YRS*

520–519 b.c. Prophesying of Haggai and Zechariah. They begin to rebuild.

515 b.c. The temple completed.

We can imagine something of the state of things if we think of a community in the present day where there is no place of worship, but where the foundations of a house of God have been laid and the people have left off building and have turned to make themselves comfortable with the very materials which they should have put in the house of God.

JOOSHA
ZERUBBABEL

B. The Analysis of the Prophecy

IN° SELF AHEAD OF THE LORD

I. The first prophecy (1:1–15). *EXHORTATION*

a. Its burden (1:1–11). The neglect of the Lord's house.
  1. Introductory (verse 1).
    (a) The date: Gentile year; Hebrew month.
    (b) The persons: The first message is to those in authority.
  2. The excuse of the people (verse 2). "The time has not come."
  3. The answer of God by Haggai (verses 3–11).
    (a) They were dwelling in their own ceiled houses (verse 4).
    (b) "Consider your ways" (verses 5–7). Thus begins and ends the section. This is a picture of long continued material failure.
    (c) The reason for failure (verses 8–11). Introduced with an appeal to build God's house. Here is distinct assertion that all the failure is God's punishment for the neglect of his house.
b. Its results (1:12–15).
  1. Obedience (verse 12).
    (a) First governor and priest.
    (b) Then the people.   *PROMISE*
  2. The word of encouragement (verse 13). "I am with you."
  3. The new enthusiasm (verses 14, 15).
    (a) The spirit of governor, priest, and people.
    (b) "They came and did work."

SIN: LOOKING BACK, INSTEAD OF AHEAD

II. The second prophecy (2:1–9). *ENCOURAGEMENT*

a. Introductory (1:1, 2).
    1. Date: About seven weeks later; the seventh day of Tabernacles. *OBSTACLE of DEPRESSION*
    2. Persons: Zerubbabel, Joshua and the people.
b. The reason of the message (1:3).
    1. Some very old men might remember (cf. Ezra 3:13).
    2. This memory tended to dishearten.
c. The message (2:4–9).
    1. The call (verses 4, 5).
        (a) The persons: Zerubbabel, Joshua and the people.
        (b) The command: "Be strong." "And work."
        (c) The promise: "I am with you"—as in the Exodus— "fear ye not." *PROMISE*
    2. The larger promise (verses 6–9). *GLORY of Temple*

Note. The central phrase of this paragraph is difficult to understand literally: "The desire (singular) of all nations shall come" (plural). The interpretation is found in the use made of the connected words in Hebrews 12:25–29. These words declare an order of divine procedure manifested both with regard to the first and second advents.
        (a) "I will shake."
        (b) The desire shall come.
        (c) The glory—material.
        (d) The greater glory—spiritual.
        (e) Peace.

Thus those disheartened on account of lesser material glory are called to look for the greater spiritual glory which is to come to the latter temple.

SIN: FAILING TO CONFESS YOUR SINS

III. The third prophecy (2:10–19). *EXPECTATION*

a. Introductory (1:10).
    1. Date: About two months later. Between this and the previous message, Zechariah had spoken his introductory word (Zechariah 1:1–6).
    2. Persons: The people are addressed through a colloquy with the priests. The content of this prophecy shows that after

three months of hard building there were not yet any signs
of material rewards (see 2:19).

b. The appeal to the priests and its lessons (2:11–13).
    1. The first question and answer (verses 11, 12). That which
       is holy cannot sanctify profane things.
    2. The second question and answer (verse 13). An unclean
       thing defiles holy things.
c. The deductions and applications (verses 14–19).
    1. The general application (verse 14).
       (a) "So"—first principle: The people now holy in their
           obedience cannot communicate cleansing to nature so
           that it will respond in full fruition.
       (b) "So"—second principle: The work of their hands hav-
           ing been unclean has contaminated and spoiled every-
           thing.
    2. Immediate application (verses 15–19a).
       (a) "Consider"—look backward to before the beginning
           of rebuilding the temple. See here the working of the
           second principle: The unfruitful work of your hands
           and the mildew and the blasting.
       (b) "Consider"—look backward from this day to the lay-
           ing of foundation of temple. See here the working of
           the first principle. Your obedience brings no resulting
           fruitfulness in nature.   *PROMISE*
d. The promise (2:19b). "From this day I will bless." The blessing
    is coming, but it is God's work.

N: UNBELIEF   IV. *The fourth prophecy* (2:20, 23).   *EXHAUATION*

a. Introductory (2:21a).
                        → *TYPE (PICTURE of Christ*
    1. Date (verse 20). The same day.
    2. Persons (verse 21). Zerubbabel. This prophecy is the en-
       forcement and explanation of the final promise of the last—
       "I will bless thee."
b. The promise (2:21b–23).
    1. Repetition of the words concerning the shaking (2:6), car-
       ried out in greater detail to reveal the destruction of all
       false power and authority (verse 22).
    2. The investiture of the governor with divine authority
       verse 23).

    (a) Zerubbabel no longer called the governor since that
        indicated Gentile supremacy.   *Promise*
    (b) "My servant." "As a signet." "I have chosen thee."
Note. The Messianic Value. (1) Literal: Matthew 1:12; Luke
3:27. (2) Positive: The coming shaking and the coming victory.

The Message of Haggai

The great message of Haggai to the people of his time was that
of the necessity for their recognition of their relationship to God
and for their expression of that recognition in the way of God's
appointment. This way was that of the temple built, and the
worship following. No excuse was to be allowed. "The time is not
come," they said, and lamented the departed glory and lack of
blessing. But even when they began the work, there were very
few results along the lines of temporal prosperity which they
expected. Against every excuse and lament the prophet appealed,
and always encouraged them with hope. When they said that
the time was not come, he said, "God is with you and therefore
the time is come." When they were lamenting the departed
glory, he told them that the God who had been with them when
they came out of Egypt was with them still and was cooperating
with them; consequently he declared that a larger glory should
come to the second temple than that which had been lost. Then
when they lamented that the material results for which they were
looking had not appeared, he told them of the ultimate victory
of God and promised that God would bless them in His own way
from that day forth. So over against all the excuses of the people
the prophet placed the perpetual reminder of the presence and
power of God, and called them to obey Him and recognize Him
and express their recognition by the building of the temple and
the setting up of worship.

C. The Permanent Message

As to the message which this prophecy brings to us today, it
seems so very patent that there is little need to more than sum-
marize it in a few sentences.

I. *Stated.* We learn, first, the sin of neglecting the divine, the sin of neglecting the outward expression of our inward belief in God. Too often men still say, "The time has not come." How many people are not doing what they ought because they are waiting for some set time. All over this country men are talking about a coming revival; it is here, if you are in earnest about it. People waiting for a future revival, if they are not careful, will miss the present workings of God. "The time has not come; it is coming." That is what these people said; and what was the result? The same thing that results today. Men are neglecting their solemn duty of building the house of God and doing the work of God while they are attending to their own business, building their own houses. Do not understand that I mean to say a word to discourage any hope or expectation, but in God's name, while you hope, work. That seems to me to be the great message of the hour. Let us by all means be strong, and let our hope be large; but the point to be insisted upon is the present duty. The one all-inclusive reason for the neglect of the things of God is the departure of the heart from God. Find what excuse you may, there is the real cause. Prosperity, especially in things spiritual, will only come as there is a return to God and attention to His work and worship.

II. Applied. But you say, "Do you really mean that we ought to build more chapels and churches?" That depends on where you live. But I can tell you one thing I mean: You have no business to go out and live in the suburbs in your ceiled house and let that old house of God downtown, where you received all the blessings of your early years, be neglected. I never see a church being pulled down to make way for hotels and theaters without my heart being sorrowful. If there are no people here, pull it down, for I have no veneration for old things that have outlived all their usefulness. But if there are immortal souls crowding into that neighborhood, you neglect it to build your own ceiled house at your peril. I know that the necessity for the temple has passed away, but I realize the importance of keeping these centers of Christian truth among the people.

There are other ways in which we do not build the temple, we say that the set time has not come. The neglect of the family altar shows a decadence in the worship of God. In all kinds of ways men are saying that they are waiting for something to come, or are lamenting something that has gone, or they are beginning to say: "We do not think it is much use anyhow; we do not see the results we would like to see." The message of God to all such is the message of Haggai. "Be strong and work, and know that I am with you. Through all apparent poverty of the hour, I am working ever on toward the final and the glorious issue upon which my heart is set." Listen to the voice of men today and then listen to the voice of God. Put these two things in contrast and you have the permanent message in this prophecy. There is a crowd of people waiting for "psychic moment," waiting for the set time. They say that they hear the wind in the top of the mulberry trees, and they lie down under the mulberry trees and wait for something else. They say there is a coming revival, and read books about it, but do not pull their coats off and go to work.

Then there are those people who are always lamenting the departed greatness, the bygone days of spiritual power; they cry for another good old-fashioned revival like that under Moody. For my part I never want to see another revival like that under Moody, never; nor like that under Finney. Why not? Because I want to have God's latest new thing. Do you not know that many men missed or were in danger of missing God's movement under Moody and Finney because they were looking to something still further back? God has some new man, and some new and better method of showing His power and His love. What we want is to be praying, not for an old-fashioned revival, but that God will accomplish His work in His own way and that He will take hold of us now and send us forth to do something. Work, and be strong to do your work. Do not sit sighing for the set time to arrive, but take hold of something and do it and give God a chance to work through you for the accomplishment of that upon which His heart is set. These are the words of the Lord through Haggai to you. "Be strong and work." And these are the words of promise, "I will shake, and I will bless, and the desire shall come."

CHAPTER 11

ZECHARIAH

1 In the eighth month, in the second year of Darius, came the word of the Lord unto Zechariah, the son of Berechiah, the son of Iddo the prophet, saying,

2 The Lord hath been sore displeased with your fathers.

3 Therefore say thou unto them, Thus saith the Lord of hosts; Turn ye unto me, saith the Lord of hosts, and I will turn unto you, saith the Lord of hosts.

4 Be ye not as your fathers, unto whom the former prophets have cried, saying, Thus saith the Lord of hosts; Turn ye now from your evil ways, and from your evil doings: but they did not hear, nor hearken unto me, saith the Lord.

5 Your fathers, where are they? and the prophets, do they live for ever?

6 But my words and my statutes, which I commanded my servants the prophets, did they not take hold of your fathers? and they returned and said, Like as the Lord of hosts thought to do unto us, according to our ways, and according to our doings, so hath he dealt with us.

7 Upon the four and twentieth day of the eleventh month, which is the month Sebat, in the second year of Darius, came the word of the Lord unto Zechariah, the son of Berechiah, the son of Iddo the prophet saying,

8 I saw by night, and behold a man riding upon a red horse, and he stood among the myrtle trees that were in the bottom; and behind him were there red horses, speckled, and white.

9 Then said I, O my lord, what are these? And the angel that talked with me said unto me, I will show thee what these be.

10 And the man that stood among the myrtle trees answered and said, These are they whom the Lord hath sent to walk to and fro through the earth.

11 And they answered the angel of the Lord that stood among the myrtle trees, and said, We have walked to and fro through the earth, and, behold, all the earth sitteth still, and is at rest.

12 Then the angel of the Lord answered and said, O Lord of hosts, how long wilt thou not have mercy on Jerusalem and on the cities of Judah, against which thou hast had indignation these threescore and ten years?

13 And the Lord answered the angel that talked with me with good words and comfortable words.

14 So the angel that communed

with me said unto me, Cry thou, saying, Thus saith the Lord of hosts; I am jealous for Jerusalem and for Zion with a great jealousy.

15 And I am very sore displeased with the heathen that are at ease: for I was but a little displeased, and they helped forward the affliction.

16 Therefore thus saith the Lord; I am returned to Jerusalem with mercies: my house shall be built in it, saith the Lord of hosts, and a line shall be stretched upon Jerusalem.

17 Cry yet, saying, Thus saith the Lord of hosts; My cities through prosperity shall yet be spread abroad; and the Lord shall yet comfort Zion, and shall yet choose Jerusalem.

18 Then lifted I up mine eyes, and saw, and behold four horns.

19 And I said unto the angel that talked with me, What be these? And he answered me, These are the horns which have scattered Judah, Israel, and Jerusalem.

20 And the Lord showed me four carpenters.

21 Then said I, What come these to do? And he spake, saying, These are the horns which have scattered Judah, so that no man did lift up his head: but these are come to fray them, to cast out the horns of the Gentiles, which lifted up their horn over the land of Judah to scatter it.

CHAPTER 2

1 I lifted up mine eyes again, and looked, and behold a man with a measuring line in his hand.

2 Then said I, Whither goest thou? And he said unto me, To measure Jerusalem, to see what is the breadth thereof, and what is the length thereof.

3 And, behold, the angel that talked with me went forth, and another angel went out to meet him.

4 And said unto him, Run, speak to this young man, saying, Jerusalem shall be inhabited as towns without walls for the multitude of men and cattle therein:

5 For I, saith the Lord, will be unto her a wall of fire round about, and will be the glory in the midst of her.

6 Ho, ho, come forth, and flee from the land of the north, saith the Lord: for I have spread you abroad as the four winds of the heaven, saith the Lord.

7 Deliver thyself, O Zion, that dwellest with the daughter of Babylon.

8 For thus saith the Lord of hosts; After the glory hath he sent me unto the nations which spoiled you: for he that toucheth you, toucheth the apple of his eye.

9 For, behold, I will shake mine hand upon them, and they shall be a spoil to their servants: and ye shall know that the Lord of hosts hath sent me.

10 Sing and rejoice, O daughter of Zion: for, lo, I come, and I will dwell in the midst of thee, saith the Lord.

11 And many nations shall be joined to the Lord in that day, and shall be my people: and I will dwell in the midst of thee, and thou shalt know that the Lord of hosts hath sent me unto thee.

12 And the Lord shall inherit Judah his portion in the holy land, and shall choose Jerusalem again.

13 Be silent, O all flesh, before the Lord: for he is raised up out of his holy habitation.

CHAPTER 3

1 And he showed me Joshua the high priest standing before the angel of the Lord, and Satan standing at his right hand to resist him.

2 And the Lord said unto Satan, The Lord rebuke thee, O Satan; even the Lord that hath chosen Jerusalem rebuke thee: is not this a brand plucked out of the fire?

3 Now Joshua was clothed with filthy garments, and stood before the angel.

4 And he answered and spake unto those that stood before him, saying, Take away the filthy garments from him. And unto him he said, Behold, I have caused thine iniquity to pass from thee, and I will clothe thee with change of raiment.

5 And I said, Let them set a fair mitre upon his head. So they set a fair mitre upon his head, and clothed him with garments. And the angel of the Lord stood by.

6 And the angel of the Lord protested unto Joshua, saying,

7 Thus saith the Lord of hosts; If thou wilt walk in my ways, and if thou wilt keep my charge, then thou shalt also judge my house, and shalt also keep my courts, and I will give thee places to walk among these that stand by.

8 Hear now, O Joshua the high priest, thou, and thy fellows that sit before thee: for they are men wondered at: for, behold, I will bring forth my servant the Branch.

9 For behold the stone that I have laid before Joshua; upon one stone shall be seven eyes: behold, I will engrave the graving thereof, saith the Lord of hosts, and I will remove the iniquity of that land in one day.

10 In that day, saith the Lord of hosts, shall ye call every man his neighbor under the vine and under the fig tree.

CHAPTER 4

1 And the angel that talked with me came again, and waked me, as a man that is wakened out of his sleep,

2 And said unto me, What seest thou? And I said, I have looked, and behold a candlestick all of gold, with a bowl upon the top of it, and his seven lamps thereon, and seven pipes to the seven lamps, which are upon the top thereof:

3 And two olive trees by it, one upon the right side of the bowl, and the other upon the left side thereof.

4 So I answered and spake to the angel that talked with me, saying, What are these, my lord?

5 Then the angel that talked with me answered and said unto me, Knowest thou not what these be? And I said, No, my lord.

6 Then he answered and spake unto me, saying, This is the word of the Lord unto Zerubbabel, saying, Not by might, nor by power, but by my Spirit, saith the Lord of hosts.

7 Who art thou, O great mountain? before Zerubbabel thou shalt become a plain: and he shall bring forth the headstone thereof with shoutings, crying, Grace, grace unto it.

8 Moreover the word of the Lord came unto me saying,

9 The hands of Zerubbabel have laid the foundation of this house; his hands shall also finish it; and thou shalt know that the Lord of hosts hath sent me unto you.

10 For who hath despised the day of small things? for they shall rejoice, and shall see the plummet in the hand of Zerubbabel with those seven; they are the eyes of the Lord, which run to and fro through the whole earth.

11 Then answered I, and said unto him, What are these two olive trees upon the right side of the candlestick and upon the left side thereof?

12 And I answered again, and said unto him, What be these two olive branches, which through the two golden pipes empty the golden oil out of themselves?

13 And he answered me and said, Knowest thou not what these be? And I said, No, my lord.

14 Then said he, These are the two anointed ones, that stand by the Lord of the whole earth.

CHAPTER 5

1 Then I turned, and lifted up mine eyes, and looked, and behold a flying roll.

2 And he said unto me, What seest thou? And I answered, I see a flying

roll; the length thereof is twenty cubits, and the breadth thereof ten cubits.

3 Then said he unto me, This is the curse that goeth forth over the face of the whole earth: for every one that stealeth shall be cut off as on this side according to it; and every one that sweareth shall be cut off as on that side according to it.

4 I will bring it forth, saith the Lord of hosts, and it shall enter into the house of the thief, and into the house of him that sweareth falsely by my name: and it shall remain in the midst of his house, and shall consume it with the timber thereof and the stones thereof.

5 Then the angel that talked with me went forth, and said unto me, Lift up now thine eyes, and see what is this that goeth forth.

6 And I said, What is it? And he said, This is an ephah that goeth forth. He said moreover, This is their resemblance through all the earth.

7 And, behold, there was lifted up a talent of lead: and this is a woman that sitteth in the midst of the ephah.

8 And he said, This is wickedness. And he cast it into the midst of the ephah; and he cast the weight of lead upon the mouth thereof.

9 Then lifted I up mine eyes, and looked, and, behold, there came out two women, and the wind was in their wings; for they had wings like the wings of a stork: and they lifted up the ephah between the earth and the heaven.

10 Then said I to the angel that talked with me, Whither do these bear the ephah?

11 And he said unto me, To build it a house in the land of Shinar: and it shall be established, and set there upon her own base.

CHAPTER 6

1 And I turned, and lifted up mine eyes, and looked, and, behold, there came four chariots out from between two mountains; and the mountains were mountains of brass.

2 In the first chariot were red horses; and in the second chariot black horses;

3 And in the third chariot white horses; and in the fourth chariot grizzled and bay horses.

4 Then I answered and said unto the angel that talked with me, What are these, my lord?

5 And the angel answered and said unto me, These are the four spirits of the heavens, which go forth from standing before the Lord of all the earth.

6 The black horses which are therein go forth into the north country; and the white go forth after them; and the grizzled go forth toward the south country.

7 And the bay went forth, and sought to go that they might walk to and fro through the earth: and he said, Get you hence, walk to and fro through the earth. So they walked to and fro through the earth.

8 Then cried he upon me, and spake unto me, saying, Behold, these that go toward the north country have quieted my spirit in the north country.

9 And the word of the Lord came unto me, saying,

10 Take of them of the captivity, even of Heldai, of Tobijah, and of Jedaiah, which are come from Babylon, and come thou the same day, and go into the house of Josiah the son of Zephaniah;

11 Then take silver and gold, and make crowns, and set them upon the head of Joshua the son of Josedech, the high priest;

12 And speak unto him, saying, Thus speaketh the Lord of hosts, saying, Behold the man whose name is The Branch; and he shall grow up out of his place, and he shall build the temple of the Lord:

13 Even he shall build the temple of the Lord; and he shall bear the

glory, and shall sit and rule upon his throne; and he shall be a priest upon his throne: and the counsel of peace shall be between them both.

14 And the crowns shall be to Helem, and to Tobijah, and to Jedaiah, and to Hen the son of Zephaniah, for a memorial in the temple of the Lord.

15 And that they that are far off shall come and build in the temple of the Lord, and ye shall know that the Lord of hosts hath sent me unto you. And this shall come to pass, if ye will diligently obey the voice of the Lord your God.

CHAPTER 7

1 And it came to pass in the fourth year of king Darius, that the word of the Lord came unto Zechariah in the fourth day of the ninth month, even in Chisleu;

2 When they had sent unto the house of God Sherezer and Regemmelech, and their men, to pray before the Lord,

3 And to speak unto the priests which were in the house of the Lord of hosts, and to the prophets, saying, Should I weep in the fifth month, separating myself, as I have done these so many years?

4 Then came the word of the Lord of hosts unto me, saying,

5 Speak unto all the people of the land, and to the priests, saying, When ye fasted and mourned in the fifth and seventh month, even those seventy years, did ye at all fast unto me, even to me?

6 And when ye did eat, and when ye did drink, did not ye eat for yourselves, and drink for yourselves?

7 Should ye not hear the words which the Lord hath cried by the former prophets, when Jerusalem was inhabited and in prosperity, and the cities thereof round about her, when men inhabited the south and the plain?

8 And the word of the Lord came unto Zechariah, saying,

9 Thus speaketh the Lord of hosts, saying, Execute true judgment, and show mercy and compassions every man to his brother:

10 And oppress not the widow, nor the fatherless, the stranger, nor the poor; and let none of you imagine evil against his brother in your heart.

11 But they refused to hearken, and pulled away the shoulder, and stopped their ears, that they should not hear.

12 Yea, they made their hearts as an adamant stone, lest they should hear the law, and the words which the Lord of hosts hath sent in his Spirit by the former prophets: therefore came a great wrath from the Lord of hosts.

13 Therefore it is come to pass, that as he cried, and they would not hear; so they cried, and I would not hear, saith the Lord of hosts:

14 But I scattered them with a whirlwind among all the nations whom they knew not. Thus the land was desolate after them, that no man passed through nor returned: for they laid the pleasant land desolate.

CHAPTER 8

1 Again the word of the Lord of hosts came to me, saying,

2 Thus saith the Lord of hosts; I was jealous for Zion with great jealousy, and I was jealous for her with great fury.

3 Thus saith the Lord; I am returned unto Zion, and will dwell in the midst of Jerusalem: and Jerusalem shall be called A city of truth; and the mountain of the Lord of hosts, The holy mountain.

4 Thus saith the Lord of hosts; There shall yet old men and old women dwell in the streets of Jerusalem, and every man with his staff in his hand for very age.

5 And the streets of the city shall be full of boys and girls playing in the streets thereof.

6 Thus saith the Lord of hosts; If it be marvelous in the eyes of the remnant of this people in these days, should it also be marvelous in mine eyes? saith the Lord of hosts.

7 Thus saith the Lord of hosts; Behold, I will save my people from the east country, and from the west country;

8 And I will bring them, and they shall dwell in the midst of Jerusalem: and they shall be my people, and I will be their God, in truth and in righteousness.

9 Thus saith the Lord of hosts; Let your hands be strong, ye that hear in these days these words by the mouth of the prophets, which were in the day that the foundation of the house of the Lord of hosts was laid that the temple might be built.

10 For before these days there was no hire for man, nor any hire for beast; neither was there any peace to him that went out or came in because of the affliction: for I set all men every one against his neighbor.

11 But now I will not be unto the residue of this people as in the former days, saith the Lord of hosts.

12 For the seed shall be prosperous; the vine shall give her fruit, and the ground shall give her increase, and the heavens shall give their dew; and I will cause the remnant of this people to possess all these things.

13 And it shall come to pass, that as ye were a curse among the heathen, O house of Judah, and house of Israel; so will I save you, and ye shall be a blessing: fear not, but let your hands be strong.

14 For thus saith the Lord of hosts; As I thought to punish you, when your fathers provoked me to wrath, saith the Lord of hosts, and I repented not:

15 So again have I thought in these days to do well unto Jerusalem and to the house of Judah: fear ye not.

16 These are the things that ye shall do; Speak ye every man the truth to his neighbor; execute the judgment of truth and peace in your gates:

17 And let none of you imagine evil in your hearts against his neighbor; and love no false oath: for all these are things that I hate, saith the Lord.

18 And the word of the Lord of hosts came unto me, saying,

19 Thus saith the Lord of hosts; The fast of the fourth month, and the fast of the fifth, and the fast of the seventh, and the fast of the tenth, shall be to the house of Judah joy and gladness, and cheerful feasts; therefore love the truth and peace.

20 Thus saith the Lord of hosts; It shall yet come to pass, that there shall come people, and the inhabitants of many cities:

21 And the inhabitants of one city shall go to another, saying, Let us go speedily to pray before the Lord, and to seek the Lord of hosts: I will go also.

22 Yea, many people and strong nations shall come to seek the Lord of hosts in Jerusalem, and to pray before the Lord.

23 Thus saith the Lord of hosts; In those days it shall come to pass, that ten men shall take hold out of all languages of the nations, even shall take hold of the skirt of him that is a Jew, saying, We will go with you: for we have heard that God is with you.

CHAPTER 9

1 The burden of the word of the Lord in the land of Hadrach, and Damascus shall be the rest thereof: when the eyes of man, as of all the tribes of Israel, shall be toward the Lord.

2 And Hamath also shall border thereby; Tyrus, and Zidon, though it be very wise.

3 And Tyrus did build herself a stronghold, and heaped up silver as

the dust, and fine gold as the mire of the streets.

4 Behold, the Lord will cast her out, and he will smite her power in the sea; and she shall be devoured with fire.

5 Ashkelon shall see it, and fear; Gaza also shall see it, and be very sorrowful, and Ekron; for her expectation shall be ashamed; and the king shall perish from Gaza, and Ashkelon shall not be inhabited.

6 And a bastard shall dwell in Ashdod, and I will cut off the pride of the Philistines.

7 And I will take away his blood out of his mouth, and his abominations from between his teeth: but he that remaineth, even he, shall be for our God, and he shall be as a governor in Judah, and Ekron as a Jebusite.

8 And I will encamp about mine house because of the army, because of him that passeth by, and because of him that returneth: and no oppressor shall pass through them any more: for now have I seen with mine eyes.

9 Rejoice greatly, O daughter of Zion; shout, O daughter of Jerusalem: behold, thy King cometh unto thee: he is just, and having salvation; lowly, and riding upon an ass, and upon a colt the foal of an ass.

10 And I will cut off the chariot from Ephraim, and the horse from Jerusalem, and the battle bow shall be cut off: and he shall speak peace unto the heathen: and his dominion shall be from sea even to sea, and from the river even to the ends of the earth.

11 As for thee also, by the blood of thy covenant I have sent forth thy prisoners out of the pit wherein is no water.

12 Turn you to the stronghold, ye prisoners of hope: even today do I declare that I will render double unto thee;

13 When I have bent Judah for me, filled the bow with Ephraim, and raised up thy sons, O Zion, against thy sons, O Greece, and made thee as the sword of a mighty man.

14 And the Lord shall be seen over them, and his arrow shall go forth as the lightning: and the Lord God shall blow the trumpet, and shall go with whirlwinds of the south.

15 The Lord of hosts shall defend them; and they shall devour, and subdue with sling stones; and they shall drink, and make a noise as through wine; and they shall be filled like bowls, and as the corners of the altar.

16 And the Lord their God shall save them in that day as the flock of his people: for they shall be as the stones of a crown, lifted up as an ensign upon his land.

17 For how great is his goodness, and how great is his beauty! corn shall make the young men cheerful, and new wine the maids.

CHAPTER 10

1 Ask ye of the Lord rain in the time of the latter rain; so the Lord shall make bright clouds, and give them showers of rain, to every one grass in the field.

2 For the idols have spoken vanity, and the diviners have seen a lie, and have told false dreams; they comfort in vain: therefore they went their way as a flock, they were troubled, because there was no shepherd.

3 Mine anger was kindled against the shepherds, and I punished the goats: for the Lord of hosts hath visited his flock the house of Judah, and hath made them as his goodly horse in the battle.

4 Out of him came forth the corner, out of him the nail, out of him the battle bow, out of him every oppressor together.

5 And they shall be as mighty

men, which tread down their enemies in the mire of the streets in the battle: and they shall fight, because the lord is with them, and the riders on horses shall be confounded.

6 And I will strengthen the house of Judah, and I will save the house of Joseph, and I will bring them again to place them; for I have mercy upon them: and they shall be as though I had not cast them off: for I am the Lord their God, and will hear them.

7 And they of Ephraim shall be like a mighty man, and their heart shall rejoice as through wine: yea, their children shall see it, and be glad; their heart shall rejoice in the Lord.

8 I will hiss for them, and gather them; for I have redeemed them: and they shall increase as they have increased.

9 And I will sow them among the people: and they shall remember me in far countries; and they shall live with their children, and turn again.

10 I will bring them again also out of the land of Egypt, and gather them out of Assyria; and I will bring them into the land of Gilead and Lebanon; and place shall not be found for them.

11 And he shall pass through the sea with affliction, and shall smite the waves in the sea, and all the deeps of the river shall dry up: and the pride of Assyria shall be brought down, and the sceptre of Egypt shall depart away.

12 And I will strengthen them in the Lord; and they shall walk up and down in his name, saith the Lord.

CHAPTER 11

1 Open thy doors, O Lebanon, that the fire may devour thy cedars.

2 Howl, fir tree; for the cedar is fallen; because the mighty are spoiled: howl, O ye oaks of Bashan; for the forest of the vintage is come down.

3 There is a voice of the howling of the shepherds; for their glory is spoiled: a voice of the roaring of young lions; for the pride of Jordan is spoiled.

4 Thus saith the Lord my God; Feed the flock of the slaughter;

5 Whose possessors slay them, and hold themselves not guilty: and they that sell them say, Blessed be the Lord; for I am rich: and their own shepherds pity them not.

6 For I will no more pity the inhabitants of the land, saith the Lord: but, lo, I will deliver the men every one into his neighbor's hand. and into the hand of his king: and they shall smite the land, and out of their hand I will not deliver them.

7 And I will feed the flock of slaughter, even you, O poor of the flock. And I took unto me two staves; the the one I called Beauty, and the other I called Bands; and I fed the flock.

8 Three shepherds also I cut off in one month; and my soul loathed them, and their soul also abhorred me.

9 Then said I, I will not feed you: that that dieth, let it die; and that that is to be cut off, let it be cut off; and let the rest eat every one the flesh of another.

10 And I took my staff, even Beauty, and cut it asunder, that I might break my covenant which I had made with all the people.

11 And it was broken in that day: and so the poor of the flock that waited upon me knew that it was the word of the Lord.

12 And I said unto them, If ye think good, give me my price; and if not, forbear. So they weighed for my price thirty pieces of silver.

13 And the Lord said unto me, Cast it unto the potter: a goodly price that I was prized at of them. And I took the thirty pieces of silver, and cast them to the potter in the house of the Lord.

14 Then I cut asunder mine other staff, even Bands, that I might break

ZECHARIAH

15 And the Lord said unto me, Take unto thee yet the instruments of a foolish shepherd.

16 For, lo, I will raise up a shepherd in the land, which shall not visit those that be cut off, neither shall seek the young one, nor heal that that is broken, nor feed that that standeth still: but he shall eat the flesh of the fat, and tear their claws in pieces.

17 Woe to the idol shepherd that leaveth the flock! the sword shall be upon his arm, and upon his right eye: his arm shall be clean dried up, and his right eye shall be utterly darkened.

CHAPTER 12

1 The burden of the word of the Lord for Israel, saith the Lord, which stretcheth forth the heavens, and layeth the foundation of the earth, and formeth the spirit of man within him.

2 Behold, I will make Jerusalem a cup of trembling unto all the people round about, when they shall be in the siege both against Judah and against Jerusalem.

3 And in that day will I make Jerusalem a burdensome stone for all people: all that burden themselves with it shall be cut in pieces, though all the people of the earth be gathered together against it.

4 In that day, saith the Lord, I will smite every horse with astonishment, and his rider with madness: and I will open mine eyes upon the house of Judah, and will smite every horse of the people with blindness.

5 And the governors of Judah shall say in their heart, The inhabitants of Jerusalem shall be my strength in the Lord of hosts their God.

6 In that day will I make the governors of Judah like a hearth of fire among the wood, and like a torch of fire in a sheaf; and they shall devour all the people round about, on the right hand and on the left: and Jerusalem shall be inhabited again in her own place, even in Jerusalem.

7 The Lord also shall save the tents of Judah first, that the glory of the house of David and the glory of the inhabitants of Jerusalem do not magnify themselves against Judah.

8 In that day shall the Lord defend the inhabitants of Jerusalem; and he that is feeble among them at that day shall be as David; and the house of David shall be as God, as the angel of the Lord before them.

9 And it shall come to pass in that day, that I will seek to destroy all the nations that come against Jerusalem.

10 And I will pour upon the house of David, and upon the inhabitants of Jerusalem, the spirit of grace and of supplications: and they shall look upon me whom they have pierced, and they shall mourn for him, as one mourneth for his only son, and shall be in bitterness for him, as one that is in bitterness for his firstborn.

11 In that day shall there be a great mourning in Jerusalem, as the mourning of Hadadrimmon in the valley of Megiddon.

12 And the land shall mourn, every family apart; the family of the house of David apart, and their wives apart; the family of the house of Nathan apart, and their wives apart;

13 The family of the house of Levi apart, and their wives apart; the family of Shimei apart, and their wives apart;

14 All the families that remain, every family apart, and their wives apart.

CHAPTER 13

1 In that day there shall be a fountain opened to the house of David and to the inhabitants of Jerusalem for sin and for uncleanness.

2 And it shall come to pass in that day, saith the Lord of hosts, that I will cut off the names of the idols out of the land, and they shall no more

be remembered: and also I will cause the prophets and the unclean spirit to pass out of the land.

3 And it shall come to pass, that when any shall yet prophesy, then his father and his mother that begat him shall say unto him, Thou shalt not live; for thou speakest lies in the name of the Lord: and his father and his mother that begat him shall thrust him through when he prophesieth.

4 And it shall come to pass in that day, that the prophets shall be ashamed every one of his vision, when he hath prophesied; neither shall they wear a rough garment to deceive:

5 But he shall say, I am no prophet, I am a husbandman; for man taught me to keep cattle from my youth.

6 And one shall say unto him, What are these wounds in thine hands? Then he shall answer, Those with which I was wounded in the house of my friends.

7 Awake, O sword, against my shepherd, and against the man that is my fellow, saith the Lord of hosts: smite the shepherd, and the sheep shall be scattered: and I will turn mine hand upon the little ones.

8 And it shall come to pass, that in all the land, saith the Lord, two parts therein shall be cut off and die; but the third shall be left therein.

9 And I will bring the third part through the fire, and will refine them as silver is refined, and will try them as gold is tried: they shall call on my name, and I will hear them: I will say, It is my people: and they shall say, The Lord is my God.

CHAPTER 14

1. Behold, the day of the Lord cometh, and thy spoil shall be divided in the midst of thee.

2 For I will gather all nations against Jerusalem to battle; and the city shall be taken, and the houses rifled, and the women ravished; and half of the city shall go forth into captivity, and the residue of the people shall not be cut off from the city.

3 Then shall the Lord go forth, and fight against those nations, as when he fought in the day of battle.

4 And his feet shall stand in that day upon the mount of Olives, which is before Jerusalem on the east, and the mount of Olives shall cleave in the midst thereof toward the east and toward the west, and there shall be a very great valley; and half of the mountain shall remove toward the north, and half of it toward the south.

5 And ye shall flee to the valley of the mountains; for the valley of the mountains shall reach unto Azal: yea, ye shall flee, like as ye fled from before the earthquake in the days of Uzziah king of Judah: and the Lord my God shall come, and all the saints with thee.

6 And it shall come to pass in that day, that the light shall not be clear, nor dark:

7 But it shall be one day which shall be known to the Lord, not day, nor night: but it shall come to pass, that at evening time it shall be light.

8 And it shall be in that day, that living waters shall go out from Jerusalem; half of them toward the former sea, and half of them toward the hinder sea: in summer and in winter shall it be.

9 And the Lord shall be King over all the earth: in that day shall there be one Lord, and his name one.

10 All the land shall be turned as a plain from Geba to Rimmon south of Jerusalem: and it shall be lifted up, and inhabited in her place, from Benjamin's gate unto the place of the first gate, unto the corner gate, and from the tower of Hananeel unto the king's winepresses.

11 And men shall dwell in it, and there shall be no more utter destruction; but Jerusalem shall be safely inhabited.

12 And this shall be the plague

wherewith the Lord will smite all the people that have fought against Jerusalem; Their flesh shall consume away while they stand upon their feet, and their eyes shall consume away in their holes, and their tongue shall consume away in their mouth.

13 And it shall come to pass in that day, that a great tumult from the Lord shall be among them; and they shall lay hold every one on the hand of his neighbor, and his hand shall rise up against the hand of his neighbor.

14 And Judah also shall fight at Jerusalem; and the wealth of all the heathen round about shall be gathered together, gold, and silver, and apparel, in great abundance.

15 And so shall be the plague of the horse, of the mule, of the camel, and of the ass, and of all the beasts that shall be in these tents, as this plague.

16 And it shall come to pass, that every one that is left of all the nations which came against Jerusalem, shall even go up from year to year to worship the King, the Lord of hosts, and to keep the feast of tabernacles.

17 And it shall be, that whoso will not come up of all the families of the earth unto Jerusalem to worship the King, the Lord of hosts, even upon them shall be no rain.

18 And if the family of Egypt go not up, and come not, that have no rain; there shall be the plague, wherewith the Lord will smite the heathen that come not up to keep the feast of tabernacles.

19 This shall be the punishment of Egypt, and the punishment of all nations that come not up to keep the feast of tabernacles.

20 In that day shall there be upon the bells of the horses, Holiness unto the Lord; and the pots in the Lord's house shall be like the bowls before the altar.

21 Yea, every pot in Jerusalem and in Judah shall be holiness unto the Lord of hosts: and all they that sacrifice shall come and take of them, and seethe therein: and in that day there shall be no more the Canaanite in the house of the Lord of hosts

ZECHARIAH—THE APOCALYPSE OF THE OLD TESTAMENT

A. THE PROPHET AND HIS TIMES

I. *Dates.* Zechariah was the son of Berechiah, the son of Iddo (1:1). In the book of Ezra he is called the son of Iddo (5:1; 6:14). From Nehemiah 12:4 we learn that Iddo was a priest and from Nehemiah 12:12, 16 that Zechariah was also a priest. If these refer to the same persons, then our prophet was also a priest. The first

part of the book is carefully dated, and the first prophetic utter-
ances of Zechariah are closely related to those of Haggai. The latter
part of the book (9—14) is undated and is of far wider application.

II. *Characteristics.* The edict of Cyrus gave the Jews the
privilege of returning to Jerusalem and of rebuilding their temple
(Ezra 1:1–4). Yet how small a remnant returned (Ezra 2). The
number was as follows:

Priests, only 4 courses out of 24.
Levites, only 74 individuals.
Singers, only 128 of family of Asaph.
Gate-keepers, only 139.
Helpers, only 392.
People, 200,000.
Slaves, 9,337.

Ezra also tells us of the desire of the Samaritans to help build
the temple, and of the refusal of the Jews to permit this. Then
followed the false reports of the Samaritans and the consequent
interference of the Persian court which interrupted the building.
This lasted for fifteen years, meanwhile the temple remained un-
finished, and the discouraged people gave themselves up to seeking
their own comfort.

This was an all-important time in the history of Israel. The
Messiah was promised to come through the chosen nation and
that nation was practically dead, and was being buried in its
captivity. How far this is true is evident by the small remnant who
had interest and enthusiasm enough to return. Through divine
intervention Cyrus issued his proclamation and the return of this
remnant was like a resurrection of the nation out of death. Thus
was made possible the coming of the Messiah.

Here is a clue to the difference between the first and the second
parts of the prophecy of Zechariah. In the first part he urges these
people to that which was of supreme importance to them as a
nation—the building of the temple—by the prophecies which
show the far-reaching effect of this work in the coming and Kingdom of the Messiah. In the latter part he deals more in detail with
certain aspects of that great future.

B. The Analysis of the Prophecy

I. The message during the building of the temple (chapters 1—8).

a. The first message (1:1-6). Complementary to Haggai.
   1. The date: About a month after Haggai's second prophecy, in which he had encouraged the people who were in danger of being disheartened by the memory of the past, Zechariah gives them another view of the past and warns them.
   2. The message.
     (a) A declaration (verse 2). Jehovah was sore displeased with your fathers.
     (b) A call (verse 3). "Return" and "I will return."
     (c) The warning (verses 4–6). "Be not as your fathers," they refused to return and the word of warning was fulfilled so that they returned later through suffering.

   Note. The value of this first message is that the prophet, from another standpoint, urges these men to be obedient to the message of Haggai. While they lament past greatness, let them remember how it was lost, and not repeat the former folly. Haggai encourages by looking forward, while Zechariah encourages by looking back.

b. The second message. Visions (1:7—6:15). Two months after Haggai's last message.

   Notes. There are three methods of interpretation of these visions. (1) That which confines their significance to the times of Zechariah. (2) That which spiritualizes very much of them by application to the Church. This method recognizes a local setting, but gives the vision a spiritual interpretation. (3) That which holds that the vision had an application to Israel but makes them refer to events yet future.

   I emphatically adopt the third method of interpretation. The first is untenable because the things declared have not been fulfilled. The attempt to explain the glorious announcement of the defeat of the foes of Israel and her victories, by the poor condition then existing and continuing until the Messiah, is to suppose the prophet guilty of the wildest and most foolish ex-

aggeration. The second method involves the exposition of the
text in inextricable and endless confusion, for there are things
that will not admit of being spiritualized and, moreover, to
apply to the Church the order and service herein revealed is to
contradict New Testament teaching as to her order and
service. The Church has a heavenly vocation, but the visions
of this book have to do with earthly, not heavenly conditions.
We shall, therefore, consider these visions as having an application to the earthly people Israel, and as yet to be fulfilled. This is the great apocalypse of God's final dealings with
Israel, and these visions represent a program of God not yet
carried out, and shows the interest of Jehovah in His people.

1. Visions of the myrtle trees (1:7–17). This is the picture
    of Israel today.
    (a) Description (verses 8, 9). (1) A man on a red horse.
        The angel of Jehovah (cf. verse 11). (2) An army on
        horses—red, sorrel and white. (3) Among the myrtle
        trees (symbols of saints). Israel. (4) In the bottom or
        shady place. Israel in oblivion.
    (b) Explanation (verse 10).
    (c) Events (verses 11–13). (1) Reports of the army to
        the angel (verse 11). (2) Plea of the angel (verse
        12). (3) Jehovah's answer to the angel (verse 13).
    (d) Commission to Zechariah—the message of Jehovah
        (verses 14–17). (1) His attitude toward Jerusalem
        and the nations (verses 14, 15). (2) His consequent
        action (verse 16.) (3) His determined victory (verse
        17).

2. Visions of horns and smiths (1:18–21). The overthrow of
    Israel's enemies.
    (a) Descriptions (verses 18–20). (1) Four horns (verse
        18). The horn is a symbol of power. (2) Four smiths
        (verse 20). The symbol of that which destroys these
        powers.
    (b) Explanation (verse 21). The horns are the powers
        which have scattered the chosen people. (2) The
        smiths are those that break the power of the horns.
    Note. This vision is indefinite as to detail, but perfectly def-

inite as to intention. God will raise up forces to destroy the
great powers that have scattered His people.

3. Vision of measuring line (chapter 2). The resultant con-
    dition of Jerusalem: restoration and prosperity.

    (a) Description (verses 1–5). A man going to meas-
        ure Jerusalem. (2) The first angel commissioned by
        a second to tell him (the prophet) of the great extent
        of Jerusalem's prosperity, and its reason.

    (b) Explanation. This is a figurative account of the great
        prosperity which is to come to Jerusalem. (1) Its
        nature: The presence of Jehovah making walls un-
        necessary. (2) Its extent: So vast prosperity as to
        make walls impossible.

    (c) Zechariah utters his consequent call (verses 6–13).
        (1) To the scattered people to return. (2) The
        declaration of Jehovah, and consequent rejoicing.

4. Vision of Joshua (chapter 3). Israel as a priest cleansed.

    (a) Description (verses 1–10). (1) Joshua the high priest
        in filthy garments before the angel of Jehovah and
        Satan: The advocate of the slanderer (verses 1–3).
        (2) Satan rebuked, Joshua cleansed (verses 2, 4, 5).
        (3) Joshua charged by the angel of Jehovah (verses
        6–10).

    (b) Explanation. (1) Israel was chosen to fulfill a priestly
        function, having access to God and mediation, but
        experienced failure resulting from sin. (2) Restora-
        tion to the fulfillment of their priestly function
        through cleansing by the mediation of the angel of
        Jehovah. (3) The charge and the promise to the
        restored nations. The coming of the Branch.

5. Vision of candlestick (chapter 4). Israel according to God's
    ideal.

    (a) Description (verses 1–3). (1) The candlestick
        (verses 1, 2). (2) The two olive trees (verse 3). (3)
        The connection between the trees and the lamp
        (verse 2).

    (b) Explanation (verses 4–14). (1) The candlestick the
        symbol of Israel as a light-bearer (verses 4–6). (2)
        The olive trees locally referred to Zerubbabel and

Joshua, the governor and the priest, but finally to the offices of priest and king which were merged in the person of Christ (verse 7). (3) Through these is communicated the Spirit through whom the light shines (verses 11–14).

6. Vision of flying roll (5:1–4). The government of the earth law.

   (a) Description (verses 1, 2). A great roll flying, twenty cubits by ten.

   (b) Explanation (verses 3, 4). The roll is the curse of evil, that is, it represents the principle of law as it will be applied by Israel fulfilling the true ideal. Evil doers will be punished.

7. Vision of the ephah (5:5–11). The restriction of wickedness.

   (a) Description. (1) The ephah—a measure (verses 5, 6). (2) Sitting in the midst of it a woman shut in by a talent of lead (verse 7). (3) The ephah lifted by two women with the wings of a stork.

   (b) Explanation (verse 8). (1) Ephah, symbol of commerce. (2) Woman, personification of wickedness. (3) The evil taken out of the nation.

Note. That the principle of wickedness is to find its final vantage ground in commerce. This is to be centralized in the land of Shinar. There the tower of Babel was erected (Genesis 10:10) and there Babylon was built. This is a revelation of the presence and the restriction of the spirit of lawlessness during millennial prosperity.

8. Vision of chariots (6:1–8). The administration.

   (a) Description: Four chariots driven from between two mountains of brass.

   (b) Explanation: The four spirits of heaven going forth from the presence of the Lord to walk to and fro in the earth. These are the administrative forces of spiritual power.

9. The great symbolic act (6:9–15). A prophecy and a picture. There emerges for the first time a priest on a throne. An historic interlude.

   (a) The preparation (verses 9–11).

(b) The prophecy (verses 12, 13).

(c) The purpose (verses 14, 15).

c. The third message. Voices (chapters 7, 8). Nearly two years later.

Introductory (7:1-7). The occasion:

(a) The date (verse 1).

(b) The question (verses 2, 3; cf. II Kings 25:8, 9, 25).

(c) The first answer: A disowning of the fasts as instituted by man, not by God (verses 4-7).

1. The word of Jehovah. First (7:8-14).

(a) Declaration of what God seeks, rather than self-appointed fasts (verses 9, 10).

(b) Declaration of their attitude (verses 11, 12a).

(c) The consequent wrath and punishment (verses 12b-14).

2. The word of Jehovah. Second (8:1-17).

(a) Restoration foretold (verses 1-8). Notice the repetition of "Thus saith. . . ." (1) I am jealous (verse 2). (2) I am returned (verse 3). (3) The result (verses 3b-5). (4) Argument and reassertion (verses 6-8).

(b) Appeal to the remnant (verses 9-13). "Thus saith."

(c) Jehovah's determination and the consequent commands (verses 14-17). (1) The determination (verses 14, 15). (2) The commands (verses 16, 17).

3. The word of Jehovah. Third (8:18-23). This is the final answer to the question suggested by the deputation (see 7:1-3).

(a) Fasts turned to feasts (verses 18, 19). The fasts were:

(1) Tenth month (II Kings 25:1). The city besieged.

(2) Fourth month (II Kings 25:3, 4). The city taken.

(3) Fifth month (II Kings 25:8, 9). The city burned.

(4) Seventh month (II Kings 25:25). Gedaliah murdered.

(b) Jerusalem the center of blessing (verses 20-23).

II. The message after the building of the temple (chapters 9—14).

a. The Burden of Hadrach (chapters 9—11). The anointed King rejected.

Note. This section is characterized by the prophet's vision of the great events in the future of his people up to their dispersion. These are all set in the light of the Kingship of Messiah. Each foretelling of an event in the history of Israel is merged into or connected with the glorious hope of the people of God.

There are three principal events foretold: (1) The coming of Alexander and the protection of the city. (2) The victory of Judah under the Maccabees. (3) The final Roman overthrow 150 years later and the scattering of the people. These events are related to the Messianic hope. The first merges into a great triumph song concerning the King who is to come, part of the prophecy contained therein having been fulfilled (9:1–10). The second passes into a description of Jehovah's triumph through His people and a lengthy description of all the blessings of His Kingdom 9:11—10:12). This Messianic section is wholly future. The third is accounted for by the rejection of the true Shepherd when He appeared (chapter 11).

1.   The King announced (9:1–10).
     (a) The preparatory preservation of the city of Jerusalem
          (9:1–8). (1) Judgment pronounced upon surrounding nations (verses 1–7). Syria: Hadrach, Damascus,
          Hamath. Phoenicia: Tyre, Sidon. Philistia: Askelon,
          Gaza, Ekron, Ashdod. (2) Protection for Jerusalem
          (verse 8).

Note. This prophecy was in large measure fulfilled two hundred years later by the coming of Alexander the Great. He captured Damascus, Sidon, and after a siege of seven months took Tyre itself. He then marched against Gaza and razed it. Though he passed Jerusalem more than once he never attacked it. Josephus gives an interesting account of the cause for this. Thus was fulfilled the prophecy contained in verse 8. The city was preserved for the coming of the King. The element of incompleteness is indicated by the sentence that "no oppressor shall pass through them any more." That was not then fulfilled, and that the prophet referred to something still more distant is proved by the fact that presently he foretells the destruction of the city.

     (b) The coming King (9:9, 10). (1) The call to joy
          (verse 9). (2) The character of the King (verse 9).

(3) The change of method adopted by the King (verse 10). (4) The climax of victory (verse 10).

2. The King's program (9:11—10:12).

(a) A coming triumph for Zion (9:11–17). (1) General announcement (verses 11, 12). (2) Particular description (verses 13–17). Judah and Ephraim used by God. Zion against Greece (verse 13). The action of Jehovah (verses 14, 15a). The consequent action of Zion (verse 15b). The united action (verses 16, 17).

Note. This prophecy was fulfilled in the victory gained by Judas Maccabaeus over Antiochus Epiphanes (165 B.C.).

(b) The King's program (chapter 10). The victory referred to suggests the great final victory. (1) The appeal to Zion. "Ask for Jehovah" (verses 1, 2). (2) Deliverance from Jehovah (verses 3–5). (3) The consequent strength and victory of His people. (verses 6, 7). (4) The King's regathering of His people (verses 8–12). "I will hiss (whistle) for them." "I will call them." "I will bring them out." "I will bring them into." "I will strengthen them."

3. The King rejected (chapter 11).

(a) The vision of judgment (verses 1–6). This is a picture of the Roman fire devouring the chosen people, and spoiling the glory of the false shepherds.

(b) The vision of the rejected King (verses 7–14). (1) His feeding of the remnant (verse 7). The two staves of the one Shepherd: "Beauty"—Grace and "Bands" —Union. The work of Jesus is twofold: love and authority. (2) His rejection of the false shepherds: or the opposing classes of rulers (verses 8, 9). (3) The rejection of the King (verses 10–14). "Beauty" cut asunder. The thirty pieces of silver (verses 10–13). The result: The breaking asunder of the "bands" between Judah and Israel (verse 14).

(c) The final judgments (verses 15–17). (1) The false shepherds restored (verses 15, 16). (2) And yet the last woe is on the worthless shepherd (verse 17).

Note. Thus the prophet sees the Roman victory over the chosen people because of their abandonment of the true King. And yet a

gleam of light is seen in that the worthless shepherd is condemned.
b.   The burden of Israel (chapters 12—14). The rejected King
enthroned.

Note. This section of the prophecy has to do with the things
wholly future. The King spoken of in the previous burden and
whose rejection is there foretold is now seen as coming into His
Kingdom. This the prophet describes in two movements, which
are complementary. In the first he is looking at the oppressing
nations as they are dealt with in judgment, and at Israel as she is
restored through the acknowledgment of her true though rejected
King, and by her own spiritual cleansing (12—13:6). In the second
he views the same events from the standpoint of the King, going
back first to His rejection, and then describing His coming day,
process and administration (13:7—14).

   1.   The final victories as to the nations and Israel (12:1—
     13:6).
     (a) As to the nations (12:1–6). (1) Strength of Jehovah
         declared (verse 1). (2) Strength of the chosen people
         determined (verses 2, 3a). (3) Strength of the nations
         discomfited (verses 3b, 4). (4) Strength of the chosen
         people discovered (verse 5). (5) Strength of the
         chosen people becomes dynamic (verse 6).
     (b) As to Israel (12:7—13:6). (1) The chosen people re-
         stored to supremacy (verses 7–9). (2) The chosen
         people recognizing their sin and repenting (verses
         10–14). (3) The chosen people cleansed (13:1–6).
   2.   The final victories as to the King (13:7—14:21).
     (a) The rejection of the King (13:7–9). (1) The shepherd
         smitten by the sword of sin (verse 7). (2) The rem-
         nant (verses 8, 9).
     (b) The day of the Lord and the King (14:1–8). (1) The
         day (verses 1, 2, 6–8). (2) The King (verses 3–5).
     (c) The process of the King (14:9–15). (1) The settle-
         ment of the land (verses 9–11). (2) The cleansing of
         conditions (verses 12–15).
     (d) The administration of the King (14:16–21). (1) The
         nations go up to worship (verse 16). (2) Absence to
         be punished (verses 17–19). (3) Consecration of all
         life (verses 20, 21).

THE MESSAGE OF ZECHARIAH

To discover the message of Zechariah to his people and to his time we must think of him as connected with that movement for the rebuilding of the temple. It is significant that out of this rebuilding of the temple which looked so mean and contemptible historically, we have this great apocalypse of the Old Testament. The prophet looks out through the centuries, and he sees and declares the result of the great things that these men were doing as they rebuilt the temple. His message was exclusively that of the absolute enthronement of Jehovah. He gives them the picture of Jehovah watching; of Jehovah acting; and of Jehovah blessing in spite of all their failure. If those people learned the spiritual value of this message they came to know that, although their condition was at the time one of poverty and almost of despair, God was watching, His armies were riding among the myrtle trees and observing, and were ever reporting to the angel of Jehovah the condition of the earth and the people. Jehovah never lost sight of the condition of His people, and although He might turn them out of their land of necessity for a while, yet He knew how to find each one of them the wide world over and knew exactly how the world was treating them. The remnant had come up to build Jerusalem and had left behind a whole company of their friends in unbelief, but Jehovah was watching over Israel even in her sin. Then the prophet says: Jehovah is not watching merely; He is at work, He is determining lines of conduct, and presently He will come to deal with the oppressor of His people, not merely because He loves His people, but because the oppressor is oppressing the only people through whom the world's Redeemer could come. He will punish the oppressor that the oppressed may be brought back to fulfill their mission, so that the love and the light of God shall stream over the whole earth. It is the picture of God acting, as well as watching, and the picture necessarily, therefore, of God's blessing.

But while that is the fundamental message of Zechariah to his people, there is also this evident teaching: The necessary attitude of the people toward Jehovah must be one of submission to His kingship, of cleansing from their pollution and, finally, of the fulfillment of His purpose of blessing others through them. The only way into blessing is by return to God's purposes and submission to them. God is on His throne, watching, acting, and He will bless, but men will only come into possession of the blessing and realization of it as they get back to Him and fulfill His purpose.

C. The Permanent Message

This prophecy, which is so largely unfulfilled, has something also to say to us. It has something to say about national life. It perfectly harmonizes with so many of the messages of the old Hebrew prophets in declaring that God is still the God of nations. When He chose Israel, He did not abandon the other nations, and in this interpolation upon times and seasons in which God is gathering out a church for heavenly work, He has not abandoned the nations of the earth; He still is the God of nations. He still girds Cyrus, though Cyrus does not know Him; He still prevents Alexander from taking Jerusalem, if He wants Jerusalem preserved. Back of all the chaos is the God of the cosmos, and through every movement of man that appears so foolish and revolutionary, anointed eyes can trace the goings of the infinite God. He has never abandoned the world or the nations of the world.

This is the deepest truth concerning national life: National greatness consists in the recognition of God and in the acceptance of His ideals. God's ideals have once been embodied and revealed to the world in the person of His King, and national greatness consists in the approximation of national ideals to the purpose and teaching of Jesus. In that magnificent work of fiction by Dr. Gunsaulus entitled *Monk and Knight*, I remember one sentence which is worth the whole price of the book, "Statesmanship is the art of finding out in what direction Almighty God is going, and in getting things out of His way." That is one of the profoundest things I have ever seen about real statesmanship. It is true. National greatness does not consist in keen, shrewd foreign policy; or in great wealth and mighty armaments. A nation is only great as it sees God behind events, and finds the way He is going, and moves along in step with Him. History demonstrates it. Is there any greatness in the American nation? Whence came it? From the fact that there were men who saw the direction in which God was going, and blazed the forests after braving the sea, to give God a chance to work out His victory. That is national greatness.

Has this prophecy a message to the Church? Yes, it reveals what her true occupation is today, but only on one side. We read the Matthew commission, the Mark commission, the Luke commission of Jesus to His disciples and the John commission, and we think they are all the same thing said in different ways. They are not. No two of them were spoken on the same occasion, and they mark different aspects of Jesus' work. The commission in Matthew, which is the Kingdom commission, does not say a word about saving men. Look this up for yourselves. "Go ye therefore and"— make disciples? No—"disciple all the nations." Then we have the individual element, "baptizing them"—not the nations, but those that obey out of them. The Church's work is not merely that of calling men to Christ; that is her first work, the winning of souls to Christ; but she has a larger work of discipling the nations; and, thank God, that work is being done. There is a Christian sentiment abroad in the world which is larger than the Christian Church. Is it not wonderful that in this day, when the latest thing that scientific thought has said to us is, "The survival of the fittest," in this very age we are more characterized than ever by the spirit that cares for the unfit? Never was there such an age for taking care of the crippled, the aged, the orphan, the demented and the wounded and sick. Is that the outcome of science? Certainly not. It is the outcome of the spirit of the Christ in the world. I thank God that Jesus is still here, and while He says to science, if I understand Him rightly, "It is quite true the survival of the fittest is natural law, but I am seeking the lost and the unfit for whom, by natural law, there is no survival." We are called to preach the gospel of salvation for the unfittest. The work of the Church, remember, is to preach this gospel, to win individual souls, and yet by her living and conduct to prepare for that moment when, her earthly work being finished, the Master will take her out to be with Himself, and will then return and find that spirit here as a preparation for His coming, which is the result of her having fulfilled her work.

What will be the effect of these convictions on the life of the Church? See how her relation to the throne of God will affect everything: her attitude toward the Jew and toward the Gentile.

Never forget that with that great apocalypse of God's purpose for Israel in view, and God's purpose for the world in view, and with this statement laid upon your conscience that the Church has to do with winning men individually to Christ and creating the very atmosphere to which the King shall presently come, do not forget that the twofold purpose of the Church in the world is best fulfilled by evangelism. It is a twofold purpose, for whenever the Church wins a man to Christ she hastens on the coming of the Lord Himself, and by the winning of that man she sets another force at work by which she witnesses to the world of the power of Christ and creates larger areas of the influence that He has exerted. Thus the Church is completed and by living men and women the influence is exerted by divine grace which prepares for the divine government.

CHAPTER 12

MALACHI

CHAPTER 1

1 The burden of the word of the Lord to Israel by Malachi.

2 I have loved you, saith the Lord. Yet ye say, Wherein hast thou loved us? Was not Esau Jacob's brother? saith the Lord: yet I loved Jacob,

3 And I hated Esau, and laid his mountains and his heritage waste for the dragons of the wilderness.

4 Whereas Edom saith, We are impoverished, but we will return and build the desolate places; thus saith the Lord of hosts, They shall build, but I will throw down; and they shall call them, The border of wickedness, and, The people against whom the Lord hath indignation for ever.

5 And your eyes shall see, and ye shall say, The Lord will be magnified from the border of Israel.

6 A son honoreth his father, and a servant his master: if then I be a father, where is mine honor? and if I be a master, where is my fear? saith the Lord of hosts unto you, O priests, that despise my name. And ye say, Wherein have we despised thy name?

7 Ye offer polluted bread upon mine altar; and ye say, Wherein have we polluted thee? In that ye say, The table of the Lord is contemptible.

8 And if ye offer the blind for sacrifice, is it not evil? and if ye offer the lame and sick, is it not evil? offer it now unto thy governor; will he be pleased with thee, or accept thy person? saith the Lord of hosts.

9 And now, I pray you, beseech God that he will be gracious unto us: this hath been by your means: will he regard your persons? saith the Lord of hosts.

10 Who is there even among you that would shut the doors for nought? neither do ye kindle fire on mine altar for nought. I have no pleasure in you, saith the Lord of hosts, neither will I accept an offering at your hand.

11 For, from the rising of the sun even unto the going down of the same, my name shall be great among the Gentiles; and in every place incense shall be offered unto my name, and a pure offering: for my name shall be great among the heathen, saith the Lord of hosts.

12 But ye have profaned it, in that ye say, The table of the Lord is polluted; and the fruit thereof, even his meat, is comtemptible.

13 Ye said also, Behold, what a weariness is it! and ye have snuffed at it, saith the Lord of hosts; and ye brought that which was torn, and the lame, and the sick; thus ye brought an offering: should I accept this of your hand? saith the Lord.

14 But cursed be the deceiver, which hath in his flock a male, and voweth, and sacrificeth unto the Lord a corrupt thing: for I am a great King, saith the Lord of hosts, and my name is dreadful among the heathen.

CHAPTER 2

1 And now, O ye priests, this commandment is for you.

2 If ye will not hear, and if ye will not lay it to heart, to give glory unto my name, saith the Lord of hosts, I will even send a curse upon you, and I will curse your blessings: yea, I have cursed them already, because ye do not lay it to heart.

3 Behold, I will corrupt your seed, and spread dung upon your faces, even the dung of your solemn feasts; and one shall take you away with it.

4 And ye shall know that I have sent this commandment unto you, that my covenant might be with Levi, saith the Lord of hosts.

5 My covenant was with him of life and peace; and I gave them to him for the fear wherewith he feared me, and was afraid before my name.

6 The law of truth was in his mouth, and iniquity was not found in his lips: he walked with me in peace and equity, and did turn many away from iniquity.

7 For the priest's lips should keep knowledge, and they should seek the law at his mouth: for he is the messenger of the Lord of hosts.

8 But ye are departed out of the way; ye have caused many to stumble at the law; ye have corrupted the covenant of Levi, saith the Lord of hosts.

9 Therefore have I also made you contemptible and base before all the people, according as ye have not kept my ways, but have been partial in the law.

10 Have we not all one father? hath not one God created us? why do we deal treacherously every man against his brother, by profaning the covenant of our fathers?

11 Judah hath dealt treacherously, and an abomination is committed in Israel and in Jerusalem; for Judah hath profaned the holiness of the Lord which he loved, and hath married the daughter of a strange god.

12 The Lord will cut off the man that doeth this, the master and the scholar, out of the tabernacles of Jacob, and him that offereth an offering unto the Lord of hosts.

13 And this have ye done again, covering the altar of the Lord with tears, with weeping, and with crying out, insomuch that he regardeth not the offering any more, or receiveth it with good will at your hand.

14 Yet ye say, Wherefore? Because the Lord hath been witness between thee and the wife of thy youth against whom thou hast dealt treacherously: yet is she thy companion, and the wife of thy covenant.

15 And did not he make one? Yet had he the residue of the Spirit. And wherefore one? That he might seek a godly seed. Therefore take heed to your spirit, and let none deal treacherously against the wife of his youth.

16 For the Lord, the God of Israel, saith that he hateth putting away: for one covereth violence with his garment, saith the Lord of hosts: therefore take heed to your spirit, that ye deal not treacherously.

17 Ye have wearied the Lord with your words. Yet ye say, Wherein have we wearied him? When ye say, Every one that doeth evil is good in the sight of the Lord, and he delighteth in them; or, Where is the God of judgment?

CHAPTER 3

1 Behold, I will send my messenger, and he shall prepare the way before me: and the Lord, whom ye seek, shall suddenly come to his temple, even the messenger of the covenant,

whom ye delight in: behold, he shall come, saith the Lord of hosts.

2 But who may abide the day of his coming? and who shall stand when he appeareth? for he is like a refiner's fire, and like fuller's soap:

3 And he shall sit as a refiner and purifier of silver: and he shall purify the sons of Levi, and purge them as gold and silver, that they may offer unto the Lord an offering in righteousness.

4 Then shall the offering of Judah and Jerusalem be pleasant unto the Lord, as in the days of old, and as in former years.

5 And I will come near to you to judgment; and I will be a swift witness against the sorcerers, and against the adulterers, and against false swearers, and against those that oppress the hireling in his wages, the widow, and the fatherless, and that turn aside the stranger from his right, and fear not me, saith the Lord of hosts.

6 For I am the Lord, I change not; therefore ye sons of Jacob are not consumed.

7 Even from the days of your fathers ye are gone away from mine ordinances, and have not kept them. Return unto me, and I will return unto you, saith the Lord of hosts. But ye said, Wherein shall we return?

8 Will a man rob God? Yet ye have robbed me. But ye say, Wherein have we robbed thee? In tithes and offerings.

9 Ye are cursed with a curse: for ye have robbed me, even this whole nation.

10 Bring ye all the tithes into the storehouse, that there may be meat in mine house, and prove me now herewith, saith the Lord of hosts, if I will not open you the windows of heaven, and pour you out a blessing, that there shall not be room enough to receive it.

11 And I will rebuke the devourer for your sakes, and he shall not destroy the fruits of your ground; neither shall your vine cast her fruit before the time in the field, saith the Lord of hosts.

12 And all nations shall call you blessed: for ye shall be a delightsome land, saith the Lord of hosts.

13 Your words have been stout against me, saith the Lord. Yet ye say, What have we spoken so much against thee?

14 Ye have said, It is vain to serve God: and what profit is it that we have kept his ordinance, and that we have walked mournfully before the Lord of hosts?

15 And now we call the proud happy; yea, they that work wickedness are set up; yea, they that tempt God are even delivered.

16 Then they that feared the Lord spake often one to another: and the Lord hearkened, and heard it, and a book of remembrance was written before him for them that feared the Lord, and that thought upon his name.

17 And they shall be mine, saith the Lord of hosts, in that day when I make up my jewels; and I will spare them, as a man spareth his own son that serveth him.

18 Then shall ye return, and discern between the righteous and the wicked, between him that serveth God and him that serveth him not.

CHAPTER 4

1 For, behold, the day cometh, that shall burn as an oven; and all the proud, yea, and all that do wickedly, shall be stubble: and the day that cometh shall burn them up, saith the Lord of hosts, that it shall leave them neither root nor branch.

2 But unto you that fear my name shall the Sun of righteousness arise with healing in his wings; and ye shall go forth, and grow up as calves of the stall.

3 And ye shall tread down the wicked; for they shall be ashes under

the soles of your feet in the day that I shall do this, saith the Lord of hosts.

4 Remember ye the law of Moses my servant, which I commanded unto him in Horeb for all Israel, with the statutes and judgments.

5 Behold, I will send you Elijah the prophet before the coming of the great and dreadful day of the Lord:

6 And he shall turn the heart of fathers to the children, and the heart of the children to their fathers, lest I come and smite the earth with a curse.

MALACHI—UNCONSCIOUS CORRUPTION

A. The Prophet and His Times

I. *Dates.* Of the prophet nothing is known more than the book reveals. The significance of his name, "my message," has given rise to the supposition that it is a title rather than a name. While believing Malachi to be the prophet's actual name, it is nevertheless significant. In this connection note his prophecy concerning John (3:1). The connection of Malachi with Ezra and Nehemiah is evident, for they refer to the same conditions.

Compare: Nehemiah 13:29 and Malachi 2:8 (polluted priesthood). Nehemiah 13:23–27 and Malachi 2:10–16 (mixed marriages). Nehemiah 13:10–12 and Malachi 3:10 (failure to pay the tithes).

Malachi begins with the cause and Nehemiah with the effect, and while Malachi is not mentioned by Ezra or Nehemiah, they deal with the same sins in the people. Probably, therefore, Malachi prophesied after Nehemiah's time.

II. *Characteristics.* The condition of things generally will be best understood by looking back over the history for about one hundred years.

536 B.C.   Return from Babylon under Zerubbabel (Ezra 3:1–4).

535 B.C.   Foundation of temple laid (Ezra 3).

520–519 B.C.   Prophesying of Haggai and Zechariah. Building resumed.

515 B.C.   Temple finished (Ezra 4:15).

458 B.C.   Ezra goes to Jerusalem with letter from Artaxerxes (Ezra 7:8).

445 B.C. Nehemiah goes to Jerusalem in the twentieth year of Artaxerxes (Nehemiah 2:1).

It would seem, then, as though the special evils which Ezra and Nehemiah set themselves to correct still existed side by side with correct outside observances. Never was the form of godliness without the power a ritual without life. The spirit of that age is revealed in the sevenfold "Wherein" (1:2, 6, 7; 2:17; 3:7, 8, 13). The prophet came to the people with a message and to every accusation they simply say, "Wherein." It is a prophecy of a stultified people, and a sensitive God. Note that this prophecy is to Israel as a "remnant including all the tribes." It is a picture of a people who imagine that they are all right where they are all wrong. They question every prophetic utterance. In this book we have the last record of an inspired utterance to Israel for four hundred years.

B. THE ANALYSIS OF THE PROPHECY

I. The fundamental affirmation (1:2–5).

a. The sensitive word of Jehovah (1:2a). "I have loved you." This the real burden of the prophecy. Everything that follows is to be viewed in the light thereof. It reveals the perpetual attitude of God and is the wail of wounded love.

b. The skeptical question of the people (1:2b). "Wherein?" A horrible and heinous blasphemy. The only explanation of such a question is that these people were conscious of the difference between their national position and their past greatness; and recognized the apparent failure of the fulfilled of the prophetic promises. It proves their blindness and hardness. They do not see that this is the cause of it all.

c. The answer of God (1:2c–5). A proof from their past history.

    1. A contrast between Esau and Jacob: Jacob loved; Esau hated.

    2. Between Edom and Israel: Edom destroyed; Israel delivered.

Note. To "hate" is used in a comparative sense in contrast to "love." (Genesis 29:30, 31; Proverbs 13:24, and Luke 14:26. Interpreted by Matthew 10:37.) The reason of the hate is to be found in the character of Esau, not in the caprice of God. If Jacob is an illustration of what God can do with a man's character, Esau is an illustration of what a man can do to shut God out of his life.

II. The formal accusations (1:6—2:17).

a. Against the priests (1:6—2:9).
    1. Their corruption declared (1:6–14).
        (a) Profanity—despising His name (verse 6).
        (b) Sacrilege—offering polluted bread (verses 7–9).
        (c) Greed.* Serving for money (verses 10, 11).
        (d) Weariness and indifference (verses 13, 14).
    2. The punishment threatened (2:1–9).
        (a) "I will curse your blessings" (verses 1–4). A terrible thing!
        (b) The true ideal of priesthood (verses 5–7).
        (c) Contempt is the punishment of corruption (verses 8–9).
b. Against the people (2:10–16). The people are specifically charged with two sins. In each case judgment is prononuced upon them.
    1. Enunciation of a principle, and declaration of a sin (verse 10).
        (a) The principle. The common relationship to God.
        (b) Dealing treacherously, and so profaning the covenant.
    2. The first sin—mixed marriage—and its judgment (verses 11, 12).
    3. The second sin—divorce—denounced (verses 13–16).
c. Against all (2:17). "Ye have wearied Jehovah with your words." If God's service wearies you, know that ye also weary him. This is a charge of accommodating doctrine to deterioration of conduct. This is generally if not always the root of heresy.

III. The final annunciations (chapters 3, 4).

a. The coming One (chapter 3).
    1. The announcement of the advent (3:1–6).

* The root idea of the Hebrew word is "without a cause," and I believe should be translated here "For naught" as in the King James version.

      (a) The person (verse 1).
      (b) The process (verses 2–5).
      (c) The principle (verse 6).
  2. The appeal to the nation (3:7–15).
      (a) General (verse 7).
      (b) The twofold charge (verses 8–15). (1) Robbery (verses 8–12). The charge; the reply and the call of love. (2) Blasphemy (verses 13–15).
  3. The attitude of the remnant (3:16–18).
      (a) The attitude described (verse 16a).
      (b) The answering attitude of God (verses 16b, 17).
      (c) The resulting determination (verse 18).
b. The coming day (4:1–3).
  1. It burneth as a furnace (verse 1).
  2. "The Sun of righteousness" (verse 2).
c. The closing words (4:4–6).
  1. "Remember Moses" (verse 4).
  2. "Will send Elijah" (verse 5). Cf. John 1:21; Matthew 17:10–13; and Luke 1:16, 17.
  3. The final word (verse 6).

The Message of Malachi

This final message of the old dispensation to Israel was first of all a message concerning God; secondly, it was a message concerning man; and thirdly, it was specifically a message to and concerning a remnant of faithful souls.

The message concerning God was a message of the constancy of His love, of the consciousness of His love, and of the courage of His love. First, of the constancy of His love. "I have loved you, saith Jehovah." That is the first word. What is the last? "Lest I come and smite the earth with a curse." Smiting the earth with a curse may be necessary, but it is not what my heart is set on. God says, "Oh, turn and remember Moses, and obey the prophet that is to come, lest I be compelled again to smite the earth with a curse." Thus the last word of the Old Testament is a sentence which is suspended by love.

Then this is a message of the consciousness of the divine love. Love is conscious of those who slight it, and of those who answer as though unconscious of their corruption. Oh, the wail of love that runs through the book: slighted love, wounded love, and yet, oh, the music of it! "The Lord hearkened," "the Lord heard," "they shall be mine . . . I will pour out a blessing upon you." It is the consciousness of love revealed, but slighted. "Bring the whole tithe into the storehouse and prove me herewith." There is only one way of proving God, and that is by giving Him love. You cannot demonstrate God by argument; you can only demonstrate Him by love. "Prove me herewith; see if I will not open the windows of heaven."

Then there is the courage of love. "Love never faileth," is written all over this last prophecy. In spite of all failure, in spite of all sin, in spite of everything, yet God will send a messenger who shall come to His temple. There shall yet be the sun of righteousness arising to bring blessing. First, he will destroy wickedness, and then, He will heal the patient, waiting souls that fear God's name. What a love song it is: the constancy, the consciousness, the courage of love!

Concerning men the prophet has a message. The prophecy reveals the failure of all motives, other than love, to maintain true relationship with God. If you serve Him from a fear of what He will do if you do not serve Him, you will soon lose your fear and your service. If you serve God on the basis of policy, you will surely fail sooner or later. There never was a more dishonest principle of action than this, "Honesty is the best policy." The man who is only honest because it is a good policy will be dishonest the moment he thinks there is an opportunity to gain by it. The man who is only loyal to God because he wants God to save him from hell, is not mean merely, but will utterly fail to be loyal to God for long. There is only one motive strong enough to maintain relationship to God: *Love*.

Now see what the death of love issues in. Callousness. "Wherein hast thou loved us?" the people asked. The prophet said: "You have lost your love for God; and now you are questioning God's love for you." That is always so; callousness results from the death of love.

Then, of course, the final message concerning man is the message of the worthlessness of form without power. God takes no interest in your words or your music unless your heart makes melody. God takes no interest in your attitude or your words when you pray unless you yourself are dealing with Him so closely that words almost become a hindrance. Externalities are nothing in themselves. You may whiten the sepulchre as you will, but you cannot attract God to communion with the dead bones within. It is the living soul, it is the loving soul, it is the power and not the form that is of worth in the eyes of God.

Concerning the remnant, what precious words the prophet delivered. He showed the true values: the Name of God. He showed them their occupation: fellowship with each other in the realm of that value. He pleaded the true hope: the coming One; and so, setting value on the Name, and having fellowship with each other, the remnant waited for the daybreak and the rising of the Sun.

C. THE PERMANENT MESSAGE

I think that none of the messages of these minor prophets fits the present age as exactly as does this of Malachi. You can take those words that I have used in referring to the message of Malachi to the men of his time, and find a message in every one of them for this day. Of God, the constancy of love, the consciousness of love, the courage of love. Of men, the failure of all other motives than love to maintain their relationship to God, the death of love always issuing in callousness, and the worthlessness of form without power.

But may I venture to apply the message in a few words? The present position of Christendom is vividly portrayed in Malachi. I very carefully use the word "Christendom," for I differentiate most carefully between Christendom and the Church. No man knows the Church of God but God Himself. You cannot tabulate the Church of God. You may take all the statistics of all the churches of all the denominations in all the world, and when you have written them all down, what have you done? You have left out a great many who are in the true Church of God, and you have put down a great many who are not really in it. I do not think the people of God ought to remain outside of the visible Church, but some of them are outside; and many members of our church organizations are not members of the invisible Church. God knows His own. But this book of Malachi gives us a true picture of

Christendom, that great mixed multitude everywhere, of people calling themselves Christians because they have an external relationship to the Church. Malachi's picture exactly fits the day in which we live. God always has His remnant, and it was never so large as it is today. But making all allowance for the company of those who do fear His name, who hold fellowship with each other, and wait for Jesus Christ, the vast bulk of Christendom has become characterized by ritual rather than by life, by form without power. Was there ever such a day of machinery as this? Was the Church of God ever so packed full in every corner with machines, machines, wheels, wheels, organizations, organizations? Yet in spite of all this machinery and activity, the heathen world is still gaining on us by leaps and bounds. Before this day has passed there will have been born unto the world more people who will live and die without the gospel than the number of those who will be brought to Christ today. That man is not courageous who shuts his eyes to the facts. All this is because the Church, taken as a whole, has form without power.

What is the message of the hour to the Church? "Behold, the day cometh." We need an understanding of the fact that the Church's true attitude was declared by Paul when he wrote his first epistle to the Thessalonians, and spoke of them as those who had turned from idols to serve God and to wait for His Son. That is the threefold truth about the Church's attitude and the attitude of every real believer in Jesus.

"Turned unto God from idols to serve a living and true God and to wait for His Son from heaven." That advent is the next event in the history of the world. Do you think it is near? I have no such words in my vocabulary concerning the methods of God as near and far. The moment you introduce an almanac or a calendar into this matter you wrong its spirit, you wrong its intention. Suppose that you could prove to me for an absolute certainty that the second advent is to take place according to the calendars of men one year from now. I would beseech of you not to tell me, because I do not want the coming of my Lord put twelve months away. I am expecting Him now, as He has commanded me. Oh, the light that breaks upon the sky when a man sees this. You ask, Are you not disappointed because He doesn't come? No, I am glad. Why? Because He does not and He knows best. Glad if He would come,

glad if He delays: that is the true attitude towards the Lord's
coming. You who bother so much about the Second Coming that
you are always thinking about it, writing about it, and talking
about it, and yet are doing nothing to save the world, hear the
message of the angels to you: "Ye men of Galilee, why stand ye
gazing up into heaven? He is coming. Get you to the work He has
left you to do." The true way to wait for the coming of the Lord is
to fill up the "little while" with evangelism in order to bring men
to Jesus Christ. I do not hesitate to say that as the final message to
the old dispensation, "Behold the day and the Sun," the final message to the new is, "Behold, I come quickly, and my reward is with
me." May I give you a very searching test to find what is your
relationship to Christ? Jesus says to you, dear child of His love,
"Behold, I come quickly." What do you reply? If you say: "Yes,
Lord, I want thee to come, but not just yet. I do want to preach
a few times more, or to do this or that first," then you are not as
near to Christ as you ought to be. Unless we are willing and waiting and hoping for Him to come and disturb us at work or at play,
we are not in the right attitude. Though all our programs be
broken and our plans be spoiled, let His program proceed and His
plan be carried out. Oh, the bright light that falls upon the pathway if we understand that He is coming!